THE POCKET BOOK OF

Civil War
Battle Sites

THE POCKET BOOK OF
Civil War
Battle Sites

From Manassas to Atlanta

ANGUS KONSTAM

CHARTWELL
BOOKS, INC.

This edition published in 2004 by
CHARTWELL BOOKS, INC.
A division of BOOK SALES, INC
114 Northfield Avenue,
Edison, New Jersey 08837

Produced by Salamander Books Limited
· The Chrysalis Building
Bramley Road, London W10 6SP

© Salamander Books Limited 2004

An imprint of **Chrysalis** Books Group

Editors: Shaun Barrington, Nikolai Bogdanovic
Designer: John Heritage
Reproduction: Anorax Imaging Ltd.
Production: Don Campaniello
All images from Salamander archives, author, Library of Congress.

ISBN: 0-7858-1920-7

Printed and bound in Malaysia

Page 1: Ohio 76th Infantry memorial, Vicksburg; Ohio played a pivotal role
in the war, with 310,654 men enrolled in 230 regiments.
Page 2: Memorial at the state Capitol building, Montgomery, Alabama.
Page 3: Pontoon bridge across the Rappahannock River below
Fredericksburg, VA.
Page 5: Wisconsin memorial, Andersonville. Almost 13,000 Federal
prisoners died there from disease, malnutrition, overcrowding, or
exposure to the elements.

CONTENTS

INTRODUCTION

Of all kinds of warfare, the Civil War is the most miserable, dividing a country and its people, and creating rifts which take generations to heal. The conflict that gripped the United States of America between 1861–65 was no exception, a fratricidal bloodbath which cost the lives of an American generation. Today the Civil War is seen as a cornerstone of American history, a period which still grips the imagination, a fact reflected in the continued popularity of period dramas set in the war, or in the sales of more serious historical studies of the conflict. What we hope to do in this book is to present the basic outline of the Civil War, as told through the battles which shaped its course. It is easy for us to divide the past into easily digestible chapters, but for those who lived through this turbulent period, the march of history shaped their everyday lives. The outcome of a battle in Tennessee could dictate the fate of millions, while the ability of the Confederate army in the east to influence international opinion could well have altered the course of American history. While we have divided the narrative by theater for the convenience of the modern reader, the reality of the conflict was that the fighting in both the east and the west were of equal importance. The fate of the entire continent depended on the outcome of either great struggle.

The issue which brought this momentous struggle to a head was the right of individual states to govern their own affairs, and the role played by a federal government. By its close President Lincoln had managed to shift the agenda, and the conflict had become more a crusade against slavery

Above: A *Federal light artilleryman's shako.*

than one of self-determination. Differences in agriculture, industrialization and slavery meant that by 1860, the differences between the North and South had become so great that Northerners and Southerners felt as if they belonged to two different countries. The Civil War has been given many names: the War Between the States, the Second American Revolution, the War of the Rebellion or the War of Secession to name just a few. This nomenclature reflects the differences that brought about the conflict, and fed resentment between the two sides, which lasted for generations after the last shot was fired. It resulted in the introduction of a powerful central government and military, the encouragement of widespread industry and big business, and the collapse of an older, more agrarian society. As with any civil war, the war was marked by ironies. Robert E. Lee became a Confederate hero only after turning down an offer to command the entire Union army. Four of

Left: *A Union naval ensign poses besides an 11-inch Dahlgren Smoothbore gun. This 16,000lb gun could launch a 130lb shell nearly a mile. The ensign's arm is resting on the gun's elevating screw.*

Lincoln's brothers-in-law fought on the Confederate side, and in Missouri, 39 regiments fought at Vicksburg: 17 on the Confederate side, and 22 fought for the Union. Above all, the Civil War was the first truly modern conflict in world history, pitting citizen armies against each other in the first war of the industrial age. It was also the most intensive conflict ever to be fought in the American continent, and the most costly.

The move to secession reached a crisis point in 1860, following the inauguration of the Republican candidate Abraham Lincoln as President. Unable to work with a politician who so strongly opposed the issues they held dear, the Southern states elected to withdraw from the Union, and created their own alliance. The Confederate States of America was as much a geographical alliance as a political one, as the marked social and economic difference between North and South meant that the South felt it had to secede in order to protect its society, and its rural way of life.

Below: *Men of a Federal horse artillery brigade near Brandy Station,* VA.

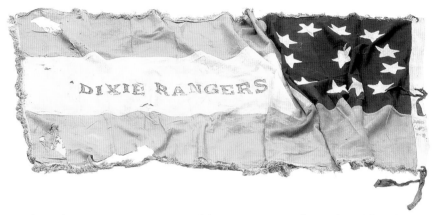

South Carolina, Mississippi, Louisiana Alabama, Georgia and Florida were the first states to break away in December 1860, followed by Texas a month later. When soldiers of this new Confederacy fired on the Union-held Fort Sumter in Charleston Harbor on April 14, 1861 President Lincoln called for volunteers to crush the "rebellion." Unwilling to fight against their fellow Southerners, North Carolina, Arkansas, Tennessee and the Commonwealth of Virginia opted to join the secessionist movement. The battlelines were drawn, and soldiers flocked to protect their new country, or to fight to re-establish the old Union by force of arms. Men like Robert E. Lee were torn between loyalty to their country, or to their state. Like many others, he elected to serve his native state, rather than take up arms against fellow Virginians. The coming war would tear America apart for four long and bloody years, and in the process Virginia would be turned into a battleground between North and South.

Above: *The Confederate first national flag carried by the Dixie Rangers.*

THE EASTERN THEATER

1st Manassas (1st Bull Run)
July 21, 1861

1st Manassas was the opening engagement of the American Civil War, and the Confederacy's first victory. Two poorly-equipped, ill-prepared armies clashed near the railroad junction at Manassas, some 25 miles southwest of Washington and 80 miles north of Richmond. Hopes for a decisive engagement proved misplaced, and the peace of the North Virginian countryside here would be shattered twice within the first 14 months of the war. The site of the battle has been preserved as a National Battlefield Park.

Right: *Civil War artillery pieces on display at Manassas National Battlefield Park.*

When news of the bombardment of Fort Sumter reached Washington, President Lincoln called for a force of 75,000 volunteers, to serve under the flag for 90 days. In the secessionist states this was seen as a virtual declaration of war, and meant that armed conflict was now inevitable. As a result, Virginia, North Carolina, Tennessee and Arkansas opted to leave the Union, while all across the South volunteers rallied to defend their homeland from attack by Lincoln's volunteer army. For the next three months no major battle would take place, but these two amateur armies would prepare for the coming battle. While the clothing and equipping of this force was a simple enough logistical

Below: *Troops under canvas at Blackburn's Ford, Bull Run.*

process in the north, the Confederacy was hard-pressed to find enough uniforms and weapons for its new volunteer army. Men took to the field in an assortment of uniforms ranging from simple homespun jackets to elaborate outfits, while still more troops took the field in their civilian clothes. President Davis even had to turn away some 200,000 volunteers, as there were no weapons to equip them with! By the summer a half million men were under arms across North America, but only 16,000 of these troops were professional soldiers from the pre-war army. The coming fight would be one that pitted one raw army against another, and the outcome would be far from predictable. It would also be discovered that the war would be neither short nor bloodless.

Lincoln adopted the grand strategy proposed by General Winfield Scott known as the "Anaconda Plan," where the Confederacy would be strangled by a combination of a rigid naval blockade (to prevent supplies reaching it from Europe) and a thrust down the Mississippi River, to cut the South in two. Equally important was the political need to protect Washington, DC and the economic necessity of protecting the North's industrial cities. While it would clearly take time to launch a major offensive in the West, the need to protect Washington dictated that the capital would see the first major troop concentration of the war. This was never seen as a purely defensive measure. As the Confederates established their own capital in Richmond, Virginia, the two centers of power were less than 100 miles apart. Both sides felt that a major drive against the enemy capital might well end the war within a matter of weeks. All that was needed was one decisive battle, fought somewhere in the rich farmlands of northern Virginia. The New York Tribune

Overleaf: *The Battle of 1st Manassas (1st Bull Run). Moving out from Centreville, McDowell's leading column under Hunter headed along the Warrenton Turnpike before crossing Bull Run at Sudley Ford. Meanwhile, Tyler headed towards Stone Bridge. MacDowell's plan worked well at first, with Beauregard taken by surprise: Evans was hard-pressed to hold the Federal masses attacking at Matthew's Hill. Meanwhile Bee and Barlow were sent to strengthen the Confederate left flank and to counterattack. Yankee pressure forced them back toward Henry Hill, until "Stone Wall" Jackson and further reinforcements stablized the line. The turning point came when Howard's Yankee brigade was caught in the flank during its attack on the Federal far right. J.E.B. Stuart delivered a demoralizing cavalry charge, and the Federal right collapsed. Federal troops streamed back across the Bull Run heading for Centreville and the safety of Washington.*

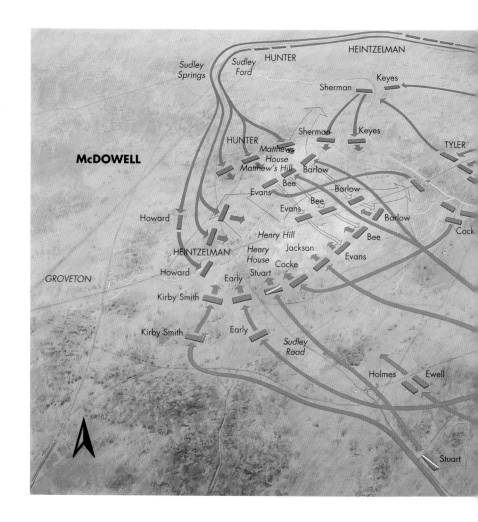

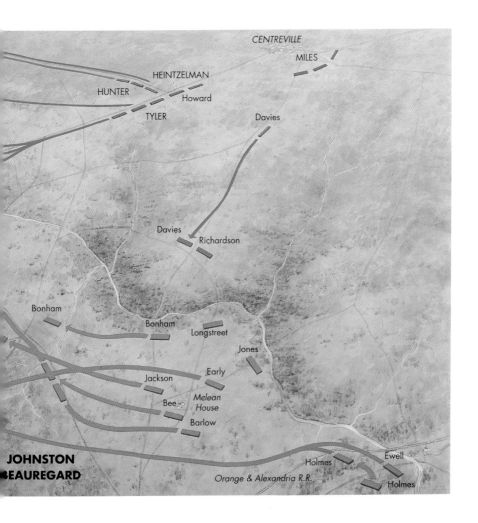

Above: A Confederate saber bayonet housed in its scabbard, from the Georgia Armory.

demanded that Lincoln's army march "On to Richmond," while its commanding officer, Major-General Irving McDowell, was reluctant to commit his raw troops to battle before they were properly trained. In the end political motives and populist demands forced the general to take the field. He tried one last plea for delay, citing the lack of training in his army. Lincoln responded; "You are green, it is true, but they are green also; you are all green alike." It was therefore decided. McDowell would invade Virginia.

In early July there were four armies in the field in the Eastern Theater. McDowell commanded 35,000 men around Washington, while another Union force of 18,000 men commanded by Major-General Patterson occupied Harper's Ferry. A Confederate force of 12,000 men under Major-General Joseph E. Johnston protected the Shenandoah Valley, while the main Confederate army, 22,000 men commanded by Major-General P.G.T. Beauregard, lay some 30 miles to the west at Manassas Junction. Clearly the main threat to McDowell's advance would come from Beauregard's outnumbered army. McDowell decided to march his army to the right, bypassing Manassas to place his troops between the two Confederate forces, and to sever Beauregard's communications with Richmond. This would force Beauregard to retreat towards Richmond, thus cutting his rail link with Johnston's smaller army to the west. Patterson's job was to advance on Johnston to prevent him from reinforcing the main Confederate army.

The advance began on July 16th. McDowell's army reached Centreville on July 18th, only to find the Confederates had pulled back behind Bull Run Creek, some two miles south of the town. A Union division was sent forward to probe the Confederate defenses near a crossing known as Blackburn's

Pierre G.T. Beauregard (1818–93)

Pierre Gustave Toutant Beauregard was born on May 28, 1818 in Louisiana. A colorful character, Beauregard had such a great admiration for Napoleon Bonaparte that he adopted the moniker "The Little Napoleon." Unlike "The Young Napoleon," General McClellan, Beauregard had enough military ability to make the name stick. He attended West Point, and graduated second in the 1838 class. He served in the Mexican–American War, then worked as an engineer until the secession of Louisiana. He offered his services to the Confederacy, and was given command of the Charleston garrison, where he supervised the firing on Fort Sumter, which began the war in earnest. For his role in the events, he earned the title "The Hero of Fort Sumter." He was then dispatched to Virginia, where he commanded the army that defeated McDowell's invading Union army at 1st Manassas. Fresh from this victory he was promoted and sent west, serving as second-in-command to General A.S. Johnston. He took charge of the Army of Mississippi after Johnston's death at Shiloh, but he fell foul of Davis, and was removed from his command. He was shipped back to Charleston, where he defended the city against naval and land assaults until the summer of 1864, when Davis had need of his services in Virginia. Beauregard held off Butler's Army above Petersburg, then moved back to the Carolinas to oppose Sherman, ending the war as General J.E. Johnston's deputy. An able but under-appreciated commander, Beauregard was one of the few commanders to successfully fight in both theaters.

Ford, but the troops were driven back before they reached the creek, and sustained heavy casualties. It was the first intimation that the coming battle would be no pushover. As soon as Beauregard realized that McDowell had begun his advance, he sent word to Johnston asking for help. Fortuitously Patterson had somehow lost his nerve, believing that Johnston outnumbered him by two-to-one. By July 18th his troops were retiring back to Harper's Ferry, and Johnston was free to reinforce Beauregard. Leaving a small division to protect the Shenandoah, Johnston embarked two-thirds of his Army of the Shenandoah onto troop trains, and sent them east to Manassas.

During the morning of July 19th the first trains carrying General Joseph E. Johnston's troops arrived at Manassas Junction, and by nightfall all 8,500 men of Johnston's force had joined Beauregard's men in their positions along the southern bank of the creek. This gave the Confederates something akin to parity of numbers with the invaders. Although Johnston was the senior commander, he agreed to let Beauregard command both armies, as his troops were already engaged with the enemy. These men had arrived in the nick of time. After the repulse at Blackburn's Ford, McDowell decided to find a way to outflank the Confederate position behind Bull Run, and sent patrols off upstream to find a suitable crossing further to the west. When word reached him that Johnston had sent troops to Manassas all plans to outflank Beauregard were abandoned. Instead he would conduct a local turning movement behind Bull Run Creek, allowing him to strike the Confederates in the flank. His decision to attack was influenced by the looming 90-day enlistment deadline. If he failed to use his army, it would simply dissolve. Three brigades under Brigadier-General

Left: *The personal memorabilia of the Confederate commander General Thomas J. Jackson. Among the items is the leather gauntlet worn by Jackson at the moment of his wounding at the Battle of Chancellorsville in May 1863. There is also a fine, cased, British-made Adams revolver with accoutrements, and a handmade, embroidered scarf presented by an admirer.*

Tyler would launch an attack across the creek at the Stone Bridge, where it crossed the Centreville Turnpike. Another brigade would make a diversionary attack further downstream at Mitchell's Ford, near the site of the skirmish two days before. Meanwhile the rest of his army (two full

JOSEPH E. JOHNSTON (1807–91)

Joseph E. Johnston was born on February 3, 1807 in Virginia. He attended West Point, graduating in 1829, and spent several years in the artillery and engineers. Johnston fought against the Seminoles and the Mexicans before he became the army's quartermaster-general. When Virginia seceded he joined the Confederates, and took command of the garrison of the Shenandoah before fighting at 1st Manassas. President Davis promoted Johnston above his rivals to command the Confederate army in Virginia, but the two did not enjoy an easy relationship, as Johnston rarely shared his plans with his commander-in-chief. He was seriously wounded in the Battle of Fair Oaks, which stopped McClellan's drive on Richmond in spring 1862, and it took a year for him to fully recover. Johnston was sent to the Western Theater, arriving too late to save Vicksburg. Elsewhere his abilities as a skilled, defensive general were tested to the limit. After Bragg's defeat at Chattanooga he relieved his subordinate of command, assuming direct control of the army facing Sherman on the borders of Georgia. Despite conducting a solid defensive campaign he was relieved of his command in front of Atlanta:the impetuous Hood took over the Confederate army defending the city. After Hood's defeat at Nashville Johnston was reinstated as overall commander in the West, and he did what he could to halt Sherman's advance through the Confederacy. On April 26th he surrendered his command at Durham, North Carolina. One of the better generals of the war, Johnston's main fault was his reluctance to take the offensive, but as a defender he was without peer.

Above: A Confederate cavalry
officer's saber and scabbard,
made by T. Griswold & Co.

divisions, commanded by Brigadier-Generals Hunter and
Heintzelman) would circle round to the west to cross Bull
Run Creek at the Sudley Springs Ford, some three miles
upstream from the Stone Bridge, and beyond the left flank of
the Confederate army. At 2am the troops began their
flanking march, and shortly after dawn on July 21st Tyler's
force launched its own attack against Brigadier-General
Evans' Confederate brigade at the Stone Bridge.

Hunter and Heintzelman managed to cross Bull Run
Creek without incident, but they found their path blocked by
felled trees, which delayed their advance. It would be 10am
before they were in a position to attack, after eight hours of
marching. Meanwhile, Beauregard was planning an offensive
of his own, an attack against the Union left across
Blackburn's Ford. He learned that Evans was under attack
from Tyler's force, but he only abandoned his planned attack
shortly after 10am, when a messenger reported that Union
troops had been seen approaching from the north along the
Sudley Springs Road. Meanwhile Evans turned his brigade
to face the new threat, deploying across the top of
Matthew's Hill. He was soon reinforced by the brigades of
Brigadier-Generals Bee and Bartow, and together the
Confederates established a strong firing line on the crest of
the hill, which temporarily halted the Union advance. Any
hope of holding the position was thwarted when Tyler
renewed his attack, sending two of his brigades across Bull
Run Creek to attack the right flank of the Confederate line,
the assault spearheaded by the brigade of Brigadier-General
William T Sherman. This attack coincided with the arrival of
Heintzelman's division on the field, which gave Hunter's
troops fresh heart. After reinforcing Hunter's troops in front
of Matthew's Hill the two divisions launched another

Above: *The flag of Co. B, 5th Regiment, South Carolina Volunteer Infantry, showing the state seal.*

Below: *The Great Seal of Virginia on a Civil War flag. The state's motto "Sic Semper Tyrannis" ("Thus Always to Tyrants") appears in the lower portion.*

assault, which took advantage of the diversion caused by Tyler. This time the Confederate line broke, the Southerners retreating back across the Warrenton Turnpike and up onto Henry House Hill beyond it. This feature was named after the house on its crest owned by Mrs. Judith Henry, an aged widow who was killed by artillery fire as the Union batteries fired in support of the advance. She thus became the first civilian casualty of the war. The time was now a little after 11am.

By this time Beauregard had realized the real threat lay to the north, and he arrived on Henry House Hill with reinforcements just in the nick of time. Their position was still desperate, as the Union advance seemed unstoppable. As the Union troops regrouped, five brigades of Confederates strung themselves out into a line behind the crest of Henry House Hill. They did not have long to wait. The center of the line was held by Brigadier-General Thomas J. Jackson's brigade from the Shenandoah Valley. As the survivors of the first Confederate line streamed past, Brigadier-General Bee tried to halt the retreat behind this line, crying; "There stands Jackson like a stone wall. Rally behind the Virginians!" Jackson had acquired a nickname. The plea worked, and the retreating troops first slowed then rallied on the southern fringe of Henry House Hill, protected by the Confederate firing line.

At 1pm, five Union brigades advanced up the hill. They were met by a wall of fire and were forced to retire, but they fell back in relatively good order to the Turnpike, and soon a second, larger assault was launched. This time the Union troops stayed on the hill and exchanged volleys with the Confederates at close range. The Confederates had the benefit of artillery support, as three batteries were deployed

Right: *George Armstrong Custer is best remembered for his famous last stand at the Little Big Horn in 1876 during the Plains Indian Wars. He graduated from West Point in 1861, finishing last in his class, but with the war approaching he was immediately commissioned. He saw his first action at 1st Manassas, going on to fight in some of the Civil War's most famous battles.*

on the hill in direct support of the battleline. McDowell decided to send forward two batteries of his own, electing to deploy them south of the Henry House, on the crest of the hill, where they could enfilade the Confederate line. They arrived shortly after 2pm. Unfortunately for McDowell the infantry regiments sent forward to support the batteries were driven back by a combination of Confederate musketry and the appearance of a small cavalry brigade under the command of Brigadier-General J.E.B. Stuart. Left unsupported, the guns were a tempting target for Jackson, who sent Colonel Cummings and the 33d Virginia forward to

Below: *The advance of the Rhode Island Brigade and the New York 71st Regiment at 1st Bull Run over the top of Matthew's Hill.*

capture the batteries. In the confusion of battle the gunners mistook the blue uniforms worn by the Virginia Regiment for those worn by their own infantry supports, and they held their fire. This misconception was shattered when the Virginians fired a volley at point-blank range, then charged. The guns were quickly overrun, and then turned on their former owners. The batteries now became the focal point of the engagement, as Beauregard sent reinforcements forward to secure the position, and McDowell launched a series of counterattacks to recapture his guns. A Union counterattack was lodged, which recaptured the pieces, but minutes later a Confederate counterattack drove the Union troops back again. The guns would change hands again during the

Above: *The flag of the 8th Regiment Viriginia Volunteer Infantry was presented to the unit by General Beauregard for valiant service at Ball's Bluff (Leesburg) in October 1861.*

Right: *Union Divisional Commander and his staff, during a modern-day reenactment of 1st Bull Run.*

course of the afternoon, but eventually it was the Confederates who ended up in undisputed possession of the batteries.

By 4pm the Union troops were exhausted, having been marching or fighting since before dawn. Inevitably their attacks began to lose momentum; shattered brigades gradually withdrew from the fight, and milled around in the valley floor on the Warrenton Turnpike. McDowell's right flank was anchored by two brigades deployed on Chinn Ridge, where Stuart's cavalry screened them. Fresh Confederate troops arriving on the battlefield were marshaled into a column by Brigadier-General Kirby Smith, then sent to attack the Union troops on the ridge. The defenders broke, retreating down the northern slope of the hill and across Young's Branch Creek to the Turnpike. By this stage the Union army had ceased to operate as a cohesive force, and it was clear that its raw troops had lost the will to continue the fight. By 5pm a steady stream of Union troops was fleeing over Bull Run Creek by the Stone Bridge, shelled by Confederate batteries sent forward to harass the Union retreat. Panic spread through the Union army, and by late afternoon the entire force was retreating over the river and back towards Washington by any means it could. Civilians who had set out that morning from Washington to witness a great victory were caught up in the headlong rout.

The exhausted Confederates were too tired to pursue, and Beauregard's army was almost as disorganized by its victory as its opponents had been by their defeat. There was no pursuit, only the slow realization that one raw army had beaten another, and that for the moment the Confederacy was saved. The battle had tested the mettle of these amateur soldiers, and it was the Confederates who emerged triumphant, producing a morale advantage that would continue to develop through a string of victories in the Eastern Theater during the years that followed. It was also clear that the war would not be settled in one single battle, but would involve the complete resources of both North and South in order to achieve victory, or to stave off defeat.

The Seven Days' Battles
June 26–July 1, 1862

In 1862 Robert E. Lee, commanding the Army of Northern Virginia, planned to drive McClellan's Federal forces away from Richmond, saving the Confederate capital. The fighting began at Mechanicsville on June 26th, a few miles northeast of Richmond. The battles were not well managed by either side, but Lee proved himself to be a trustworthy and tenacious leader. Parts of the Beaver Dam Creek and Gaines Mill battlefields have been preserved and are today maintained by the Richmond National Battlefield Park Service.

Right: *Major-General George B. McClellan, wearing the light sash in the center of the photograph, and staff.*

The Battle of 1st Manassas demonstrated that victory for the North would be a harder prospect than first imagined. In the weeks that followed, President Lincoln signed enlistment bills that authorized the raising of an army of 1,000,000 volunteers, whose terms of enlistment were not for a set period, but for the duration of the war. Recruits flocked to sign up, and in late July the new Army of the Potomac was created, under the command of Major-General George B. McClellan. He was a promising

commander whom the press named "The Young Napoleon," but whose real talents lay more in organization than strategy or martial prowess. In November 1861 McClellan was promoted to command all Union forces. He proved to be an excellent administrator and used his skills to turn the raw Army of the Potomac into an efficient military force. He was also reluctant to commit his new army to the field, but when prompted he developed a plan to transport it by sea around the flank of the Confederate army at Manassas, which was

Left: *Artillery pieces. The artillery of both combattants was quite similar. The more popular types were the Ordnance rifle (far left), Parrot rifle, and the smoothbore "Napoleon," fabricated by both sides in various configurations. The Confederate artillery also used many obsolete pieces updated by binding and rifling. The Model 1841 6-pounder field gun (far right) was used by the Union artillery while the 12-pounder Dahlgren boat howitzer (center) was issued to their navy.*

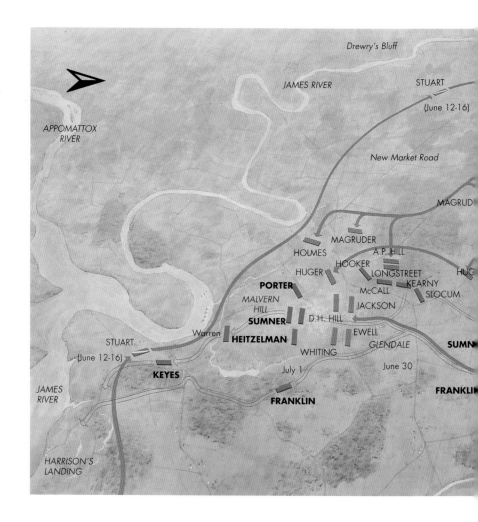

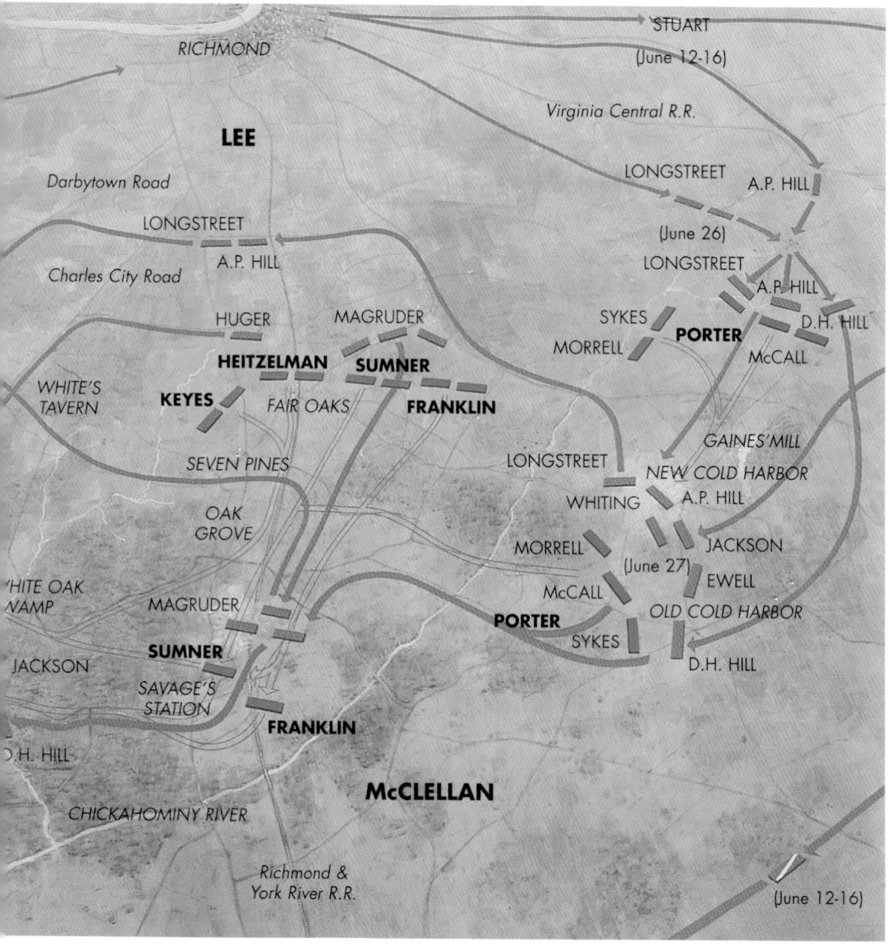

RICHMOND

STUART
(June 12-16)

Virginia Central R.R.

LEE

Darbytown Road

LONGSTREET
A.P. HILL

LONGSTREET

A.P. HILL

(June 26)

Charles City Road

LONGSTREET

HUGER

MAGRUDER

A.P. HILL

D.H. HILL

SYKES

MORRELL

PORTER

McCALL

HEITZELMAN

SUMNER

WHITE'S
TAVERN

KEYES

FAIR OAKS

FRANKLIN

SEVEN PINES

GAINES' MILL

LONGSTREET

NEW COLD HARBOR

WHITING

A.P. HILL

OAK
GROVE

MORRELL

JACKSON

HITE OAK
VAMP

MAGRUDER

McCALL

(June 27)

EWELL

OLD COLD HARBOR

JACKSON

PORTER

SYKES

SUMNER

D.H. HILL

SAVAGE'S
STATION

D.H. HILL

FRANKLIN

McCLELLAN

CHICKAHOMINY RIVER

Richmond &
York River R.R.

(June 12-16)

Previous pages: *The Seven Day's Battles. Lee struck first at Beaver Dam Creek, then again at Gaines' Mill on June 27th. Neither of these brought about a decisive victory. On June 29th he failed to crush the divided Yankee army at Savage's Station, and the next day he struck again at Glendale. McClellan slipped the trap and positioned himself on Malvern Hill. Lee's attempt at a full frontal assault here was repulsed at heavy cost, but McClellan withdrew.*

Above: *The forage cap of Lieutenant-Colonel William Fowler, 146th New York (Zuoave) Regiment.*

now commanded by the very able General Joseph E. Johnston. This would place McClellan between Johnston and Richmond. However, Johnston moved his army back to Fredericksburg shortly before the operation began, so McClellan revised his plans, selecting an even more ambitious operation, which involved landing under the guns of the Union stronghold of Fort Monroe overlooking Hampton Roads, on the tip of Virginia's Tidewater Peninsula.

McClellan's army embarked from Alexandria, across the Potomac from Washington, and on April 3rd the troops landed at Hampton Roads. The following day the blue columns began their march up the Peninsula, advancing towards a small Confederate force blocking their way at Yorktown. These 15,000 Confederates were commanded by General John B Magruder, whose orders were to delay any attacker for as long as he could. He managed this admirably: by marching and countermarching his troops, he convinced McClellan that the enemy force he was facing was far larger than it was in reality. McClellan decided to lay siege to Yorktown, an operation which involved the preparation of siegeworks, the bringing up of his heavy guns and mortars, and a delay of four weeks while everything was prepared. This bought time for the Confederates, allowing Johnston's army to march south from Fredericksburg to Yorktown. A day before McClellan's bombardment was due to begin, Johnston and Magruder slipped out of their entrenchments and escaped, leaving McClellan to claim victory after occupying their abandoned positions. Despite a rearguard action fought at Williamsburg on May 5th, the Confederate retreat continued unimpeded, and a week later Johnston's men had crossed the Chickahominy River and were entrenched in front of Richmond. McClellan pursued as best

George B. McClellan (1826–85)

George Brinton McClellan was born in Philadelphia on December 3, 1826. His father was a doctor, and his family wealthy. He entered West Point in 1842 at the tender age of 15, and did well there. He graduated second in his class in 1846. Following his graduation, he served in the Corps of Engineers, and fought in the Mexican War. After the war, he returned to West Point as an instructor, and also spent time in Europe and the Crimea, observing how European armies functioned. Nicknamed "The Young Napoleon" by the press and "Little Mac" by his men, McClellan took command of the Union army following the defeat at 1st Manassas in July 1861; much was expected of him. He told the press he expected to march to Richmond and overwhelm the Confederates in a single battle. While his plan to transport the army to the Virginia peninsula was audacious, his handling of the army during the Peninsular Campaign that followed was little short of atrocious. A key fault of his was an over-cautious assessment of the enemy's strength, and poor tactical execution. He allowed himself to be surprised by General Johnston at Fair Oaks, then was forced to retreat by General Lee during the Seven Days' Battles. Although he was stripped of overall command of the Union army he retained control of the Army of the Potomac. After General Pope's defeat at 2nd Manassas, McClellan regained the confidence of the President, but his subsequent mismanagement of the Battle of Antietam finally cost him his command. He sought revenge by running against Lincoln as a Democrat during the 1864 election, but was soundly defeated.

he could, but progress was slow. He established his supply base at White House Landing on the Pamunkey River, where he could use the Richmond and York River Railroad to bring up the supplies he needed for his final advance on the Confederate capital. He deployed his corps on both sides of the river, keeping troops on the north bank to facilitate a link with McDowell's corps, which had occupied Fredericksburg and was expected to march south to join the main army. However, the maneuvers of "Stonewall" Jackson in the Shenandoah Valley meant that rather than reinforce the army in front of Richmond, McDowell's men were ordered to halt, then send reinforcements to help counter Jackson.

Johnston realized that the division of McClellan's army presented him with an opportunity, so on May 31st he launched an attack against Brigadier-General Keyes' IV Corps encamped in the vicinity of Fair Oaks and Seven Pines,

Below: *A Union camp at Centreville, Virginia.*

on the south side of the Chickahominy River. His original plan called for a pincer movement, but poor staff work meant that the Confederates were committed piecemeal. Although Keyes' corps was all but destroyed in the Battle of Fair Oaks, the Confederates failed to achieve the crushing victory they anticipated, largely because Union reinforcements arrived to prop up McClellan's shattered defense. Worse still, just before nightfall Gerald Johnston was shot and seriously wounded, depriving the Confederates of their commander. The following day (June 1st) the attack

resumed. By this time, however, the Union defenders were too numerous to shift, and a Union counterattack drove the Confederates back to their starting positions by noon. Both sides lost around 5,000 men killed and wounded during the fighting, but the engagement served to make McClellan even more cautious, and he refused to advance until Washington sent him more troops. Even more significantly, President Jefferson Davis selected General Robert E. Lee to command the Confederate troops in front of Richmond, a force which was duly renamed the Army of Northern Virginia, a name it would retain throughout the war.

Lee's first action was to order his men to dig earthworks, an action which earned him the nickname "King of Spades."

Above: *Soldiers of the Army of the Potomac look down on their encampment on the Pamunkey River, May 1862.*

Above: *The uniform and effects of Major-General George G. Meade. These include a Model 1839 Topographical Engineer officer's saber and scabbard made by N. P. Ames, Springfield, Massachusetts. The officer's slouch hat was worn by Meade during the Battle of Gettysburg in July 1863. The silver forks, made by Filley and Mead, are from a mess set used by Meade during the Mexican and Civil wars.*

In fact Lee was securing his frontline, establishing a strong defensive position between the Chickahominy River and the White Oak Swamp, which could be held by a relatively small force. Next, Lee ordered his cavalry commander, Brigadier-General J.E.B. Stuart, to reconnoiter McClellan's positions. On June 12th Stuart led 1,200 Confederate cavalry north and east, riding around the right flank of the Union army and penetrating deep into its rear. After crossing the York River Stuart headed south, evading his pursuers by crossing the James River. He then rode west to return to Richmond in triumph. This dramatic and cavalier achievement helped to boost the morale of Lee's army, and gave him the information he needed to plan the counterattack that would drive the invaders from the gates of Richmond.

Lee planed to concentrate his army on the north bank of the Chickahominy River, and then to attack Brigadier-

George G. Meade (1815–72)

George G. Meade was born to an American family in Cadiz, Spain, on December 31, 1815. Meade attended West Point and graduated from there in 1835. He fought as an artillery officer in the Seminole War in Florida, before resigning to work as a civil engineer for the US government. He rejoined the army in 1842 prior to the outbreak of the Mexican–American War, and served as a topographical engineer. With the start of the Civil War, he served in the Army of the Potomac as a brigade commander, then a divisional commander, and was rewarded for his stalwart service by promotion to corps commander in December 1862, on the eve of the Battle of Fredericksburg. He displayed sufficient aggression during the otherwise disastrous battle that he was feted by the newspapers. In June 1863 he was ordered to replace General Hooker as commander of the Army of the Potomac, a post he held for the rest of the war. Meade fought Lee to a standstill at Gettysburg; his victory was achieved by his mastery of defensive tactics, and his eye for terrain. He pursued the defeated Confederate army back into Virginia, but his lack of aggression made Lincoln wary of his new commander. Rather than replace him, Grant decided to accompany Meade's headquarters during the 1864 campaign, like "an admiral aboard his flagship." As a result it was Grant rather than Meade who was seen as the real commander of the army, even though Meade remained a competent and popular leader. After the war, Meade commanded the Division of the Atlantic, and was put in charge of one of the Reconstruction districts. Meade died in Philadelphia on November 6, 1872.

General Porter's V Corps, which was isolated there, while the rest of McClellan's forces lay south of the river. Overall the Confederates were outnumbered two to one, but this move gave Lee superiority in numbers where it mattered. Jackson defeated the last Union force in the Shenandoah Valley on July 9th, and as a result his 18,000 men were available to join the main army. Jackson's men were duly transported across the state and on the evening of June 26th, when Lee's planned attack was due to get underway, the Army of the Shenandoah was a short day's march to the north of Porter's right flank. On the afternoon of June 26th Lee launched his assault; the men of Major-General A.P. Hill's division passed through the village of Mechanicsville to assault Porter's defensive position behind Beaver Dam Creek. Two other Confederate divisions (those of D.H. Hill and Longstreet) remained in reserve, leaving Magruder and Major-General

Below: *At the start of the Seven Days' campaign, the Union army was divided by the Chickahominy River.*

Huger with 25,000 men to guard Richmond. Unfortunately, Jackson's men never appeared, and Hill's men were repulsed after making a costly frontal assault. As night fell Porter was convinced he could hold his position, but McClellan was worried about Jackson attacking Porter's flank, and ordered V Corps to fall back under cover of darkness, to take up a new defensive position six miles to the east, behind Boatswain's Creek. While Porter was fighting Hill north of the river, McClellan launched a series of limited assaults against Magruder's defenses, but did nothing to support V Corps. However, he did order the transfer of his supply base from the White House to Harrison's Landing on the James River. This was a defensive move; it demonstrated that McClellan was convinced he faced a more numerous enemy, and was obsessed with saving his troops rather than capturing Richmond or defeating Lee.

Above: M Battery, 2d US Artillery, near Fair Oaks, June 1862. The battery, commanded by Captain Benson, fought at Malvern Hill on July 1. Benson was later killed there.

Above: *The Union positions behind Beaver Dam Creek at Mechanicsville, viewed from the Confederate side of the creek.*

On the morning of June 27th Lee continued his march across Beaver Dam Creek and on to Gaine's Mill. Porter's men lay a little further to the southeast. This advance was a gamble, as a concerted Union attack south of the river could well have led to McClellan capturing Richmond. McClellan made no such move, and by the early afternoon Lee's army stood before Porter's position. In the Battle of Gaine's Mill that followed, Lee launched a series of frontal assaults on Porter's line, first using A.P. Hill's division, and then Longstreet's. Jackson arrived during the late afternoon, and his troops were launched into the attack, supported by the division of D.H. Hill. Initially the defenders managed to hold off these attacks, but shortly after 4.30pm Porter's line was breached by Brigadier-General Hood's Texas Brigade. Confederate reinforcements then swept over the crest above the creek and drove the shattered Union line back in retreat. The Union withdrawal was covered by McClellan's artillery,

and by a spirited but suicidal cavalry charge. Lee's first victory of the campaign cost him 8,000 men killed or wounded—twice the casualties inflicted on Porter's corps. However, the battle convinced McClellan that he had no chance of holding Lee, and consequently he ordered his army to retreat towards its new supply base at Harrison's Landing. This hard-fought victory had saved Richmond.

On the following day neither army was engaged, as Lee was unsure where McClellan had gone; meanwhile the bulk of the Army of the Potomac was marching south, preceded by a vast column of supply wagons en route from White House to Harrison's Landing. While Stuart's cavalry probed eastward towards the abandoned Union supply base, Lee moved his divisions south of the river, the majority moving in a sweep westwards through Richmond, to strike the retreating Union army in the flank. On June 29th Lee ordered Magruder and Huger to join the advance, and they probed

Above: *State markers and military trail markers cover the battlefields of Virginia.*

Above: Two Civil War-era canteens, one made of wood (above) and one of tin (below). Both designs had drawbacks. The tin canteen would eventually rust, while the wooden one needed waxing inside to prevent leakage.

forward, clashing with the Union rearguard at Savage's Station, but failing to pin down the Union defenders north of the White Oak Swamp. By the following morning McClellan's army was protected by this long line of marshy ground, and he took up positions south of the Swamp at White Oak Swamp Bridge, and at the crossroads of Glendale. While Jackson appeared north of the Swamp and did nothing more than trade artillery shots across the destroyed bridge, Longstreet (commanding his own division and that of A.P. Hill) had marched southeast from Richmond, and came upon the Union army blocking his path between White Oak Swamp and the James River. He launched an immediate attack, and in the action known as the Battle of Frayser's Farm (or Glendale), McClellan managed to hold off this Confederate assault, buying time for his supply train to complete its journey. Unsupported by Jackson and Huger, who had moved up in support, Longstreet achieved little, and suffered heavy casualties. That evening McClellan's army broke away to the south, and by dawn on July 1st had established itself in a strong defensive position at Malvern Hill. The Union fleet on the James River protected the army's rear, a steep bluff protected its western flank, and its front was covered by McClellan's massed guns. Porter masterminded the defense, while McClellan headed for Harrison's Landing. Confederate attempts to bring up artillery to pound the Union position were thwarted by concentrated counterbattery fire. Lee launched a series of frontal attacks throughout the day, none of which even reached the Union line, each being repulsed by heavy fire. Darkness ended the bloodbath. Porter saw this defensive victory as an opportunity to strike Lee's demoralized army, but McClellan ordered him to continue the retreat to the

Above: *A battle-damaged artillery piece.*

James River. By the following morning Harrison's Landing had become a virtually impregnable fortress, and the Army of the Potomac was saved, having been bundled south by the smaller Army of Northern Virginia. Lee's audacious plan had worked, but this hard-fought victory came at a cost. The Confederates lost nearly 20,000 men during the week-long campaign, a quarter of the army, but Union casualties were equally extensive, and the Southerners had achieved a spectacular strategic success. The war would continue, but Richmond would remain secure until the very end of the war.

2nd Manassas (2nd Bull Run)
August 29–30, 1862

At 2nd Manassas, Robert E. Lee established himself as the Confederacy's most effective commander, while John Pope lost his reputation and most of his army. Lee's hard-fought victory opened the way for an invasion of Maryland, an attempt to take the war out of the battered farmlands of Virginia and to inflict defeat on the enemy on their own soil. Today the site is preserved within the confines of the Manassas National Battlefield Park, comprising some 5,000 acres.

Right: *Gen. John White Geary (center) was one of several effective Union commanders from Pennsylvania. At Lincoln's call to arms he had organized the 28th Pennsylvania Infantry that fought at the battle.*

While the Peninsular Campaign was still underway, President Lincoln and Union Secretary of War Edward Stanton tried to consolidate the Union forces elsewhere in Virginia. To command them Lincoln selected Major-General John Pope, a commander who had achieved moderate success in the Western Theater, and of whom both the President and Stanton entertained high hopes. He assumed command of these troops on June 26th, the day Robert E. Lee launched his counterattack against the Army of the Potomac which would become known as the Seven Days' Battles campaign. Pope designated his new command of 45,000 men the "Army of Virginia."

In early July Pope pushed his army south from its headquarters at Manassas, his leading units crossing the Rappahannock River to reach Culpeper Courthouse. His objective was to capture Gordonsville 25 miles to the south, which would sever the Virginia Central Railroad linking Richmond to the Shenandoah Valley. However, Lee's successes around Richmond coupled with McClellan's lack of aggression meant that Lee was soon free to despatch troops to deal with the threat posed by Pope's army. On July 19th Jackson arrived in Gordonsville with his Army of the Valley, a force of 12,000 men. He soon discovered that Pope had split his army into its three constituent corps, and these troops were strung out along the line of the Orange and Alexandria Railroad between Orange Courthouse (ten miles north of Gordonsville) and Manassas. The closest Union formation was the corps commanded by Major-General Nathaniel Banks—8,000 men who were occupying Culpeper Courthouse. Banks had orders to probe to the south, but it was Jackson who moved first, leading his army north across the Rapidan River on August 9th to intercept Banks at Cedar

Mountain, a few miles south of Culpeper. In the battle that followed Jackson found himself under attack from the smaller Union army facing him, but victory was assured when Ewell's Division arrived on Banks' left flank, forcing his men to retire. Union losses in the battle were 2,381 killed or wounded, but Banks' army remained a useful force, while Jackson lost 1,276 men and the element of surprise. Pope now knew that Confederate forces were operating to his front.

For days later Jackson's army at Culpeper Courthouse was reinforced by the arrival of Major-General Longstreet, who brought 11,000 men with him. This allowed the army to be divided into two powerful corps-sized groups. On August 20th the Confederates crossed the Rappahannock and advanced as far as Jeffersonton, where Lee joined his army with reinforcements, bringing the total Confederate strength up to 55,000 men, some 10,000 more than Pope had available to him. Lee knew that the Army of the Potomac had been ordered to embark from the Peninsula and travel by steamer to Aquia Creek, where it would march overland to support Pope. McClellan was unwilling to do anything to help his rival in command, so he delayed his advance for as long as possible. This benefited Lee, who was able to concentrate his entire force against Pope. He called his commanders together and proposed an audacious move designed to inflict a decisive defeat on Pope before McClellan could

Above: *The Federal Major-General Winfield Scott Hancock (seated) with (from left to right) Franics Barlow, David Birney and John Gibbon. Hancock was one of the best Union corps commanders in the Army of the Potomac, and would persuade Meade to fight at Gettysburg.*

arrive to reinforce him. The plan called for Jackson to take his corps on a wide flank march to emerge behind the Union army, and Jackson welcomed the proposal. His force set out on the morning of August 25th, marching westward to Amissville before heading north some 20 miles to Salem, arriving shortly after nightfall. The following day Jackson led his men east past Gainesville to emerge behind Pope's rear at Bristoe Station, a few miles south of Manassas Junction. Jackson's men had covered 54 miles in less than two days. This move cut Pope's line of communications to Washington along the Orange and Alexandria Railroad. The first Pope knew of this was when word reached him that a large Confederate force had derailed one supply train, and caused a second to run into the wreckage of the first. Jackson then learned of an enormous Union supply depot outside Manassas, and his men were sent to plunder what they could. The soldiers were amazed by what they found; including tinned lobster salad, weapons, coffee and blankets. That evening (August 26th) they looted what they could, and destroyed the rest. Pope's army was concentrated

Below: *The Confederates held the high ground at 2nd Manassas, just behind these trees. 10,000 Union troops attacked Jackson across these fields, and were bloodily repulsed.*

on the railroad some ten miles south of Bristoe Station, near Warrenton. He immediately marched his entire army north to confront the raiders. It was only when he clashed with Ewell's rearguard at Bristoe Station during the afternoon of August 27th that he realized he was facing Jackson. Rather than be concerned, the confident Pope saw this as an opportunity to isolate and crush a significant part of Lee's army. Warned of Pope's approach, Jackson destroyed the railroad bridge over Bull Run, then deployed his force along the line of an unfinished railroad, just north of the Warrenton Turnpike, west of Bull Run Creek, and some eight miles northeast of Manassas. The railroad embankment formed a natural defensive position running along the forward slope of Sudley Mountain, from Sudley Church to a position just north of Groveton, on the Warrenton Turnpike. If he was to fight a defensive battle he could hardly have selected a better position, but an even greater benefit was

Above: *A Union sharpshooter, drawn for* Harper's Weekly *by the war correspondent* Winslow Homer *in Virginia,* 1862.

Above right: *The fading traces of the unfinished railway embankment just north of the Warrenton Turnpike, which Jackson used as an earthwork.*

provided by the fact the disposition of his army was hidden from Pope, who would have to probe along the Confederate line to find a weak spot.

Pope ordered two of his three widely dispersed corps, Sigel's I Corps and McDowell's III Corps, to concentrate on Manassas Junction. He was also able to drawn upon some reinforcements from the Army of the Potomac; Reynold's Division detached from V Corps, Heinzelman's III Corps and elements of the newly-created IX Corps under the command of Brigadier-General Reno. Porter's fast-marching V Corps had already reached Bristoe Station from Aquia Creek. Shortly before nightfall on August 28th the units on Jackson's right engaged part of McDowell's corps around Groveton. All this achieved was to let Pope know where Jackson was, and the Union commander ordered Sigel's I Corps to attack and pin down Jackson the following day, while the rest of the army marched to the sound of the guns. Unfortunately while Pope might have been able to control his own troops, he relied on McClellan to hasten his own units forward in support. Instead "Little Mac" tried to delay his advance, so that Pope would bear the full brunt of the fighting. The logic behind this was that any failure on Pope's part could only help salvage McClellan's battered reputation.

Early on August 29th Schurz's Division of Sigel's Corps attacked Jackson's line near Sudley Church, but was repulsed, despite the support of Kearny's Division of Heinzelman's Corps. On the far left another Union probe was repulsed by point-blank artillery fire along the Groveton–Sudley Road. It was still not even 10am. By this stage the advanced units of Longstreet's command were reaching the battlefield, the first of which, Hood's Division, deployed across the Warrenton Turnpike between Gainesville and Groveton. Both sides were now sending all available troops to join the fight. As Longstreet's men arrived, they began to drive back the Union divisions waiting in the woods south and west of Groveton, but Longstreet (now joined by Lee) held the bulk of his army in check until it was fully in position. Meanwhile Pope ordered McDowell to attack Jackson's right flank near Groveton, ostensibly supported by Porter's V Corps of McClellan's army. The veteran Porter ignored these orders, and formed a line facing Longstreet, an action that would later lead to him becoming the scapegoat for Pope's failure. McDowell joined the Union forces massing for a general assault against Jackson's line, including Reno's IX Corps and Heinzelman's III Corps of the Army of the Potomac. These troops launched their attack all along the line shortly after 3pm, but in most places the attackers were driven back. The exception was in the center, where the men of Hooker's Division of III Corps drove through the center of Jackson's line along the railroad.

Above: *Confederate belt plates. The letters on the upper plate stand for South Carolina, and the lower sword-belt plate shows the Virginia state seal.*

Unsupported, they were eventually forced to retire in the face of determined Confederate counterattacks. This small success made Pope think that he had gained the upper hand, and that Jackson planned to withdraw to the west. Pope ordered Hatch's Division of McDowell's Corps to advance down the Warrenton Pike to head Jackson off, but all he did was to run into Hood's Division outside Groveton, and the Union formation was badly mauled in the last fighting of the day.

Both sides remained in place during the night, and the battle resumed at dawn on August 30th. Lee continued to hold Longstreet back, hoping Pope would pin his army against Jackson's line. This is exactly what happened. A sequence of attacks by 10,000 Union troops was launched on Jackson's right, a portion of the railroad line known as "The Deep Cut." Jackson's line held, and Porter's attackers were driven back with heavy losses, pursued by Starke's Division of Jackson's army. McDowell sent Reynold's Division to block their path, and these troops deployed in line along Matthew's Hill, supported on their right by Reno's Corps. This left just 2,200 Union troops to the south of the Warrenton Turnpike. It was the moment Lee had been waiting for. He ordered Longstreet to launch his attack, and shortly after 4pm 25,000 Confederates drove east towards the Sudley-Manassas Road. While the handful of Union troops in the area fought a determined rearguard action, they were unable to stop the wave of Confederate troops, despite Pope's hurried redeployment south of the Turnpike. As darkness fell the Union defenders had been pushed back onto Henry House Hill, the scene of another Confederate victory the year before. Jackson's men joined in the general advance, putting pressure on the hastily-formed Union line

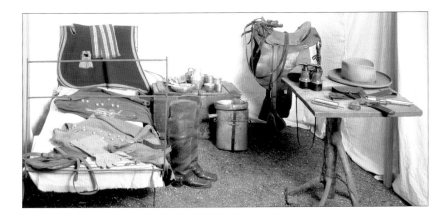

on Matthew's Hill and forcing it back across the Sudley–Manassas Road. At 6pm Pope ordered a general withdrawal east of the road, where a second line was formed as darkness fell. The following day Pope's army withdrew across Bull Run Creek and headed back to the safety of Washington. The demoralized Union troops even began to talk of the battle as "their annual Manassas whipping." The battle cost Lee 9,474 men, but Pope lost 14,462, his reputation and his army. Within days he was stripped of his command, and McClellan was restored as commander of all Union forces in Virginia. Although he may have lacked aggression, he was a gifted administrator, and he already had experience of rebuilding an army shattered at Manassas. For Lee his hard-fought victory opened the way for an invasion of Maryland, an attempt to take the war out of the battered farmlands of Virginia and to inflict a decisive victory over the enemy on their own soil.

Above: *The personal possessions of General Robert E. Lee. Among the items shown are a camp bed and blanket used by Lee during the siege of Petersburg in 1864, and a table used at the winter headquarters near Orange Courthouse during 1863–64. The pen shown was used to sign the surrender at Appomattox in 1865.*

Antietam (Sharpsburg)
September 17, 1862

The events of September 17, 1862 constitute the Civil War's bloodiest day. More casualties were recorded here than anywhere else during the conflict. The North's strategic victory, halting Lee's advance into Maryland, brought home the full horror of the "War between Brothers" to the wider public, as the Army of Northern Virginia fought for its life. The Antietam battlefield is located 14 miles south of Hagerstown, Maryland. The remains of Confederate trenches can still be seen, and it is one of the best preserved battlefields of the war.

Right: *Abraham Lincoln, holding onto the chair, poses with General McClellan (directly facing him) and other Federal commanders at Antietam.*

Following his victory at 2nd Manassas the initiative in the Eastern Theater passed to Robert E. Lee. One option was to adopt a defensive position, waiting for the next Union invasion, but this would surrender the initiative to the enemy. Instead Lee chose to take the war to the North by crossing the Potomac River into Maryland. This would spare the farmland of Virginia further ravages, and might encourage the European governments to recognize the Confederacy. Although McClellan, now restored to command of the Union forces in the Eastern Theater, could draw upon an army of 84,000 men, Lee felt with justification that his 55,000-strong Army of the Potomac was its equal due to their experience and superior morale.

Screened by the cavalry of J.E.B. Stuart, the Army of Northern Virginia crossed the Potomac River at White's Ford near Leesburg on September 4th, then advanced north towards Frederick, Maryland. Knowing that a majority of Marylanders supported the Southern cause, Lee's army was

Below: *Then and now. The Dunker Church, site of some of the heaviest fighting at Antietam.*

on its best behavior. The army reached Frederick on September 7th, by which time word of the invasion had reached Washington, and McClellan readied his army to march to engage the enemy. At this point Lee divided his army into three columns, with his instructions for the operation laid down in "Special Order No. 191,". The first column of three divisions under "Stonewall" Jackson was to march west, re-cross the Potomac at Williamsport, Maryland, then turn south to isolate the Union garrison of 12,000 men at Harper's Ferry. The division of John C. Walker was to take up a position on the Maryland side of the Potomac facing Harper's Ferry, thus cutting off the town from

Below: *The bodies of Confederate soldiers lie ready for burial at Antietam. The Dunker Church is in the background.*

Right: *Burnside's Bridge, viewed from Confederate positions on the north bank of the Antietam Creek.*

reinforcements. Finally Major-General McLaws was ordered to take the two remaining divisions in the army and block the passes over South Mountain, a range spreading south through Maryland to the Potomac near Harper's Ferry that cut the state in two. Together with Stuart's cavalry, this force would protect the rear of the army while Jackson completed his investment. Two days later he modified this deployment on discovering that a Union force of unknown strength lay west of South Mountain at Hagerstown, Marlyand. By sending Longstreet's Division to investigate, his army became even more dangerously scattered. This was a reasonable gamble given McClellan's record of inertia. However, on September 13th a copy of "Special Order No. 191" was brought to McClellan's headquarters at Frederick: a Confederate had used it to wrap cigars, and then dropped the small package. McClellan now realized just how vulnerable Lee's army was. With uncharacteristic alacrity he

Ambrose E. Burnside (1824–81)

Ambrose Burnside was born on May 23, 1824. He attended West Point, graduating in 1847. He spent six years in the artillery, serving in Mexico and New Mexico. He resigned in 1853, and attempted to make his fortune by designing a breech-loading carbine—a financial disaster for him personally. He also held a post as a major-general in the state militia. Burnside was simply promoted beyond his abilities. As one contemporary put it: "Few men have risen so high on so slight a foundation." He commanded a brigade of Massachusetts volunteers at 1st Manassas, and then operated independently, winning several easy victories on the Carolina coast. Following his return to Washington, he was given command of a corps in the Army of the Potomac, and commanded it with courage, if not distinction, at Antietam. However, Burnside enjoyed strong political support, and he assumed command of the Army of the Potomac following McClellan's removal. He led the army to disaster at Fredericksburg in December 1862, launching 14 ill-co-ordinated assaults on an impregnable Confederate position, and losing 9,000 men in the process. He was replaced as army commander, but was given another chance as a Corps commander in Meade's army. However, he led this corps in another bungled attack in the Battle of the Crater outside Petersburg. He was sent on leave and never recalled, and he resigned in 1865. After the war, Burnside concentrated on his business affairs. He was elected as Governor of Rhode Island three times between 1866 and 1868, and was a Senator from 1875 until his death on September 13, 1881.

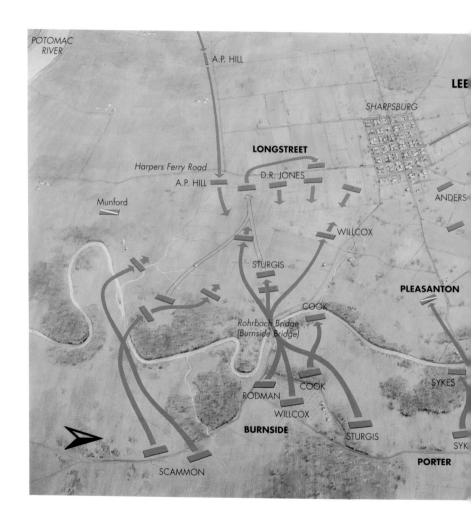

POTOMAC
RIVER

A.P. HILL

LEE

SHARPSBURG

LONGSTREET

Harpers Ferry Road
A.P. HILL

D.R. JONES

ANDERS

Munford

WILLCOX

STURGIS

PLEASANTON

COOK

*Rohrbach Bridge
(Burnside Bridge)*

COOK

SYKES

RODMAN

WILLCOX

BURNSIDE

STURGIS

SYK

SCAMMON

PORTER

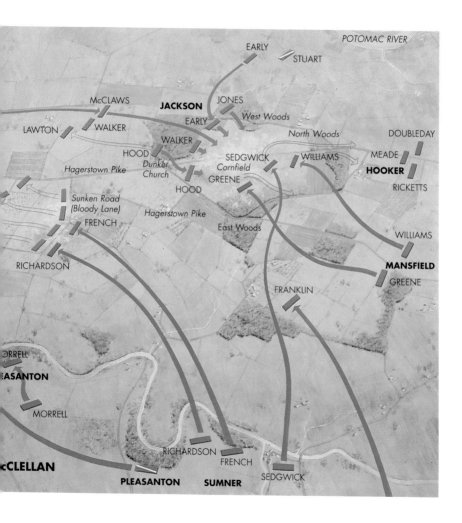

Previous pages: *Hooker's Corps crossed the creek and pushed into North Wood and the infamous Cornfield. Meanwhile, II Corps under Sumner crossed the creek to Hill's outnumbered Confederates at the Sunken Road. At late-morning, Burnside began his attempts to cross the creek, squandering his men at the Rohrbach Bridge. He finally made it across in late afternoon, but was stopped by A.P.Hill's counterblow at Harpers Ferry. Hill's move saved the Army from almost certain destruction. Reinforcements pushed Burnside back almost to the bridge. Battle was suspended at nightfall. Lee withdrew on the night of the 18th.*

Right: *Manning a redoubt built on the battlefield of Fair Oaks outside Richmond. McClellan first demonstrated his hesitancy during the Seven Days Campaign. At Antietam it cost him the chance of inflicting a decisive victory.*

gathered his army, issued orders and sent it forward towards South Mountain.

Warned of McClellan's advance, Lee ordered his army to concentrate near Sharpsburg, to the west of South Mountain. Meanwhile Longstreet was ordered to move up in support of McClaws at South Mountain. On September 14th D.H. Hill fought a spirited delaying action at South Mountain, holding off two full Union divisions who tried to force the pass at Turner's Gap. Two miles to the south, at Crampton's Gap, McClaws held off Franklin's Corps. These two actions bought time for Lee to concentrate his army, and that night Hill and McClaws withdrew to join the rest of the army. Meanwhile Jackson had reached Harper's Ferry,

and on September 15th the town surrendered, yielding 12,000 prisoners. Leaving A.P. Hill's Division behind to secure the town, Jackson led the rest of his force northwards to join Lee at Sharpsburg. Lee lacked sufficient troops to have any real chance of beating McClellan. His goal was survival, but outnumbered four-to-one and with his back to a large river, he found himself in a tough position. At least Jackson's arrival would give Lee's 19,000 men a fighting chance of holding off McClellan's 87,000-strong army, until Lee could disengage his force and withdraw back across the Potomac. Fortunately for him Jackson's men arrived during the night; four veteran divisions, which brought the Confederate numbers up to 40,000 men. Lee was still outnumbered by more than two-to-one.

McClellan decided to launch a series of attacks against Lee's flanks, hoping his opponent would weaken his center in order to strengthen his wings. Then McClellan could smash his reserve of Porter's veteran V Corps into Lee's center. While a laudable plan, it wasted his great advantage of numbers. A co-ordinated Union attack all along the line would almost certainly have overwhelmed Lee's army, but this piecemeal approach would press the Confederates rather than break them. Shortly after dawn on September 17th, McClellan launched Major-General "Fighting Joe" Hooker's Corps against Lee's left. Hooker advanced southward through the North Wood, spearheaded by Meade's Division. As they crossed a cornfield they were subject to the full fire of J.R. Jones' Division. Despite horrendous casualties Hooker managed to drive Jones back into the West Woods before a counterattack by Hood's Division pushed the attackers back beyond the cornfield. Hooker sent in his reserves, and for a while the cornfield

Above: *A Confederate bugle with attachments for a carry strap.*

Above: *The sunken lane at Antietam. This was filled with the dead of both sides after the battle.*

became a bitterly contested battleground. However, at 7.30am Major-General Mansfield's raw XII Corps attacked over the same ground; again the fighting here at the cornfield was savage and bloody, but this time Hood's men were unable to repulse the Union onslaught. By 9am the Union troops had managed to push the Confederate line back a half-mile to the Dunker Church, placing Lee in a dangerous position with a powerful enemy force on his flank. By this time Hood had lost almost two-thirds of his force, while Hooker's Corps had lost one-third of its strength and the survivors were too exhausted to continue in support of XII Corps. Only the intervention of D.H. Hill staved off a Confederate defeat, and the attackers were forced to give ground, easing pressure on Lee's defenders. Somehow the

Confederate line held. Major-General Sumner had been requesting orders to advance since the fighting began, and finally at 10am he was allowed to attack. He sent Sedgwick's Division over Antietam Creek towards the left-center of the Confederate line near Dunker Church, but he was met by the fire of McClaws' Division; they then charged Sedgwick in the flank, driving his men off to the north where they rallied in the North Woods. In the fighting that followed, Mansfield was killed, but McClaws' men were forced to withdraw back over the contested ground to their original positions near Dunker Church.

The battle now moved to the south. Sumner still had two more divisions; those of French and Richardson. These now attacked the Confederate centre, where the attackers were met by D.H. Hill's Division, redeployed along a sunken road that later became known as "The Bloody Lane." French attacked first, but were unable to carry the strong Confederate position, despite suffering heavy casualties. Instead they fired over the sunken lane at Confederates sent forward to reinforce Hill's line, the men of R.H. Anderson's Division. Next it was Richardson's turn. Once again the attackers endured heavy losses, but this time they were able to carry part of the position, driving some of Hill's men back towards Sharpsburg. McClellan has been criticized for not sending Porter's V Corps into the fight at this point, as these extra troops would have almost certainly broken the battered Confederate line. To ease the pressure, Longstreet gathered an ad-hoc force and attacked French's right flank to the north of the sunken lane, forcing French to pull back a little. This helped save the day in the center, as Richardson's Union division was now unsupported. Despite a final attack by men of Franklin's Corps in the direction of the West

Woods, the Confederates managed to hold their ground throughout the early afternoon, and Richardson was eventually forced to withdraw.

As the fighting died down in the north and center of the battlefield, McClellan increased the pressure from the south. The Union IX Corps, commanded by Major-General Burnside, had spent the early part of the battle waiting for orders, but shortly after 10am Burnside was told to advance over the stone bridge crossing Antietam Creek to his front, and to drive the Confederates back into Sharpsburg a mile beyond the bridge. He was promised support from Porter's Corps once he had secured a bridgehead. Several attempts were made to storm the bridge, but each time the attackers were repulsed by Confederate fire from the bluff overlooking the bridge. Snavely's Ford lay further downstream, so Burnside sent Rodman's Division to seize this and turn the Confederate position. This would take time, so in the meantime Sturgis' Division of Porter's V Corps launched a fresh attack across the stone bridge. This time the attackers managed to make it across, largely as the defending Georgians of Toombs' Brigade were low on ammunition. By 1pm Burnside had his bridgehead; Sykes' Division of V Corps crossed the Middle Bridge to offer him support as planned. Meanwhile Rodman's Division appeared, and Burnside prepared to launch an attack towards Sharpsburg, defended by D.R. Jones' Division. At 3pm he advanced, but the right flank of the Union wing was checked by artillery fire from Cemetery Hill to the east of Sharpsburg. Sykes could have cleared this position, but instead held his men back as he had no orders to attack. Rodman had more success on Burnside's left, charging through the units on Jones' right flank. It was now 5pm, and the way to Sharpsburg lay open.

At that critical moment a fresh body of troops appeared on Burnside's left. It was the men of A.P. Hill's Division, who had force-marched from Harper's Ferry to join the battle. They charged, and rolled up the Union flank, forcing Burnside to retreat back across the Creek. This ended the bloodiest day in American history. Lee's army had survived to fight again, but the cost was high: 10,319 men killed, wounded or missing, just over 30% of the army. Union losses were even higher: 12,400 men, or 25% of the troops committed to the fight. McClellan had missed a perfect opportunity, and his failure cost him his command. Shortly after he visited the battlefield, Lincoln stripped McClellan of his command, and handed command of the army to Ambrose Burnside. Meanwhile Lee led his army back into Virginia, and prepared for the next Union invasion.

Below: *The New York State Monument erected in 1919, located to the north of the Visitor Center. A quarter of the Union army at Antietam came from New York.*

Fredericksburg
December 13, 1862

Burnside's winter campaign against the Confederate capital of Richmond involved the capture of the strategically important town of Fredericksburg. However, the events on the Rappahannock River would prove to be his undoing. The futile assault on Marye's Heights by no fewer than 14 successive Federal brigades and Longstreet's defense of the stone wall have entered Civil War legend. Today the battlefield is preserved within the Fredericksburg and Spotsylvania National Military Park, Virginia.

Right: *Zouaves of the 114th Pennsylvania Infantry, photographed in August 1864. The 114th participated in the Fredericksburg, Chancellorsville, Gettysburg, and Petersburg campaigns.*

Following Antietam, Lee took up a defensive position on the south bank of the Rappahannock River, and waited for the Army of the Potomac's next move. On November 7, 1862 Major-General Ambrose Burnside assumed command of the army, and immediately reorganized it into three "grand divisions" under major-generals Sumner, Hooker and Franklin. He planned to outmaneuver Lee by marching south from the army's base near Manassas towards Fredericksburg, and to force a crossing of the Rappahannock River before Lee could react. The army began its move on November 15th, and two days later its leading units had reached Falmouth, a small town on the north and east bank of the river opposite Fredericksburg. He discovered the town was held by just 500 men, and Lee was still a day's march to the west, while Jackson was still in the Shenandoah Valley. Although all the bridges over the river had been destroyed, Burnside's men could have gathered boats and crossed in sufficient numbers to drive away the defenders in the town. An immediate crossing would have placed the Army of the Potomac between Lee and Richmond. Burnside had planned to throw pontoon bridges over the river and send his army across, but the bridges had still not arrived, having been delayed at Manassas on the orders of General Halleck, Burnside's superior, who was reluctant to commit the army to operations south of the Rappahannock. Consequently Burnside's army waited for another week, by which time Lee had arrived, and his troops had begun digging in along the heights above the town. The Union army had lost the element of surprise.

A more cautious general would have called off his planned river crossing, but Burnside was determined to take to the offensive. He devised a plan that called for a

simultaneous crossing by two "grand divisions" (each of two Corps.) The first involved a crossing at Fredericksburg itself by Sumner's wing, which would pass through the town to attack Lee's positions on Marye's Heights to the west. Further downstream Franklin's wing would cross 1.5 miles below the city, then march southwest to take the long line of Prospect Hill, ground now held by Jackson's Corps. To affect this maneuver, three pontoon bridges were to be placed across the river at Fredericksburg, and three more at Hamilton's Crossing, where Franklin would cross.

Above: *Unable to dislodge the Confederates from the heights above Fredericksburg, the Union had to content itself with a long-range bombardment of the Confederate lines during the first months of 1863. Officers examine the effects of this bombardment after Union troops occupied the area in May.*

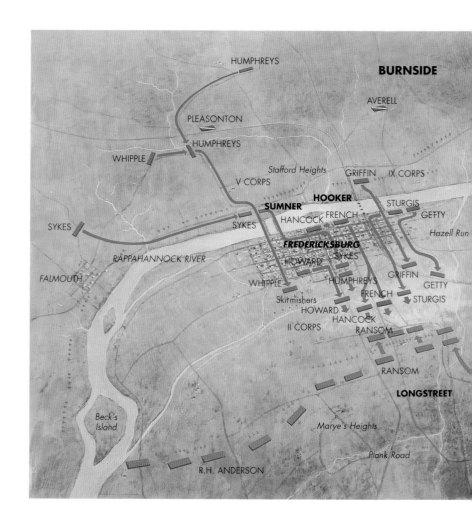

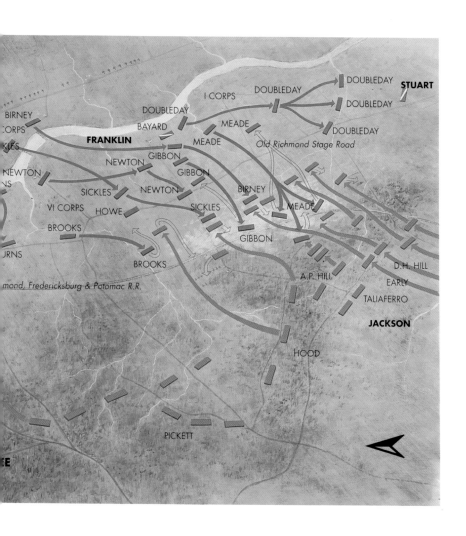

BIRNEY
CORPS
KLES
NEWTON
NS
SICKLES
NEWTON
VI CORPS HOWE
BROOKS
URNS
BROOKS
mond, Fredericksburg & Potomac R.R.

FRANKLIN
BAYARD
DOUBLEDAY
NEWTON
GIBBON
GIBBON
SICKLES

I CORPS
MEADE
MEADE
BIRNEY
MEADE
GIBBON

DOUBLEDAY
DOUBLEDAY
DOUBLEDAY
DOUBLEDAY
STUART
Old Richmond Stage Road

A.P. HILL
HOOD

D.H. HILL
EARLY
TALIAFERRO
JACKSON

PICKETT

E

Previous pages: *The Federal attack at Fredericksburg played into Lee's hands. The Confederates were given plenty of time to position themselves prior to the battle, as the Federal forces attempted to bridge the Rappahannock. Meade's initial assault on the Rebel positions accomplished nothing, and II Corp's attack up the gradual slope to Marye's Heights was met by a wall of fire. The Federal forces pressed on with their attack until nightfall, but each successive wave was repulsed, and not one bluecoat made it to the stone wall in front of the heights. Burnside retired across the Rappahannock two days later. His foolishness had cost the Union side over 12,000 casualties, compared to Lee's much lighter losses of some 5,000 troops, and he was soon relieved of his command.*

Confederate sharpshooters harassed the Union engineers building the bridges, so progress was slow until Sumner sent troops across the river in boats to drive off the Confederate riflemen. It took almost three weeks to complete the bridges, but by the second week in December everything was in place. At dawn on December 13th Sumner's men began crossing the river, the morning mist hiding their actions from the Confederates on the heights above the town. His men formed up in the open ground outside Fredericksburg, and then began to advance towards Marye's Heights, held by McClaw's Division of Longstreet's Corps, supported by the divisions of Hood, Pickett and Ransom. The Confederate position was a strong one; the troops in the front line were protected by Telegraph Road, a sunken lane lined by a stone wall, while the Confederate guns were deployed above them, where they could sweep the ground to the front of the Confederate positions. Shortly after noon Sumner's first line approached this position, and came under heavy artillery fire. The ground was broken by ditches, making progress slower than Sumner expected. The artillery fire increased as the troops approached the stone wall, and by the time the Confederate infantry joined in the fire was devastating. Whole regiments were cut down in their ranks by the wall of fire, and the attack faltered. Sumner's second line moved forward, only to meet the same fate. The Confederates, arrayed six deep behind the stone wall were relatively safe, harassed only by long-range Union artillery fire from across the river. Throughout that long winter afternoon Sumner made repeated attempts to take the Confederate position, but no attacker ever reached closer than 100 yards from the stone wall. By mid-afternoon it was clear that the attack was an abject failure, as it had already

JOSEPH HOOKER (1814–79)

Joseph "Fighting Joe" Hooker was born in Hadley, Massachusetts, on November 13, 1814. He attended West Point, graduating in 1837, and went on to serve in the Seminole and the Mexican–American wars. In 1855 he resigned his commission following an argument with Winfield Scott, the army's general-in-chief. He took up farming in California, and only returned to the army after the disaster at 1st Manassas. He was given command of a brigade in the Army of the Potomac, and led it with flair during the Peninsular Campaign, in the course of which he was promoted to major-general, and emerged as a divisional commander. His reputation was somewhat marred by his drinking, but this failed to prevent him being given control of a corps in time for the Antietam Campaign, where he was one of the few Union commanders to emerge from the battle with his reputation intact. After the debacle at Fredericksburg his open criticism of Burnside led to the removal of the commander, and Hooker found himself in charge of the Army of the Potomac. He led the army in one campaign, but after launching a promising operation he seemed to lose his nerve at Chancellorsville, surrendering the initiative to Lee, and allowing his opponent to outmaneuver him. Hooker was duly replaced by Meade. He was sent west, where he fought with great aplomb at Lookout Mountain near Chattanooga, but resigned in the middle of the Atlanta Campaign, as he refused to serve under Thomas. Hooker was famous for being a prickly and argumentative character (hence the nickname "Fighting Joe".) He died in New York on October 31, 1879.

Above: *Following Meade's unsuccessful assault, Burnside directed the right of his line to attack through Fredericksburg. The Federals had to advance up these daunting, bare slopes to Marye's Heights.*

cost Sumner 8,000 men. Those who survived the slaughter hugged whatever cover they could find, and prayed for the cover of night when they could retreat in safety. Watching from the heights above the scene, Lee remarked; "It is well that war is so terrible. Men would love it too much."

On the Union left the attack was slightly more successful. Franklin delayed crossing the river until after 10am, and it was not before noon that his lead division commanded by Major-General Meade approached Prospect Hill. Although his 50,000 men gave Franklin a clear numerical superiority over Jackson he allowed his advance to be delayed by harassing artillery fire from his left flank. This came from just two guns of Major Pelham's Horse Artillery, supported by Major Walker's main guns on Prospect Hill itself. Franklin waited until the Confederate batteries were neutralized by Union counter-battery fire, then he pressed forward across the line of the Richmond, Fredericksburg & Potomac Railroad. Rather than concentrate his attack on Jackson's right flank, Franklin's "grand division" veered slightly to the right, as a wooded march lay in its chosen path. This change of plan actually worked in Franklin's favor, as Major-General Meade's attack was launched directly at the one weak spot in the Confederate line. Longstreet had deployed a division on either side of the morass, but no troops were positioned across it apart from a thin skirmish line detached from Hood's Division. Realizing this, Meade marched his division into the boggy gap, his advance supported on his right by Brigadier-General Gibbon's Division. Purely by chance the Union attack also directed itself at the spot where Longstreet and Jackson's commands met, making it harder for the Confederates to launch a concerted counterattack. The Union formations were able to plunge through the gap in the Confederate frontline, then advance uphill into the trees to engage Lane's Brigade of A.P. Hill's Division, which was broken. The Union advance continued into Jackson's reserves, deep in the Confederate rear. The Confederates were taken by surprise. One regiment from South Carolina was overrun and largely captured *en masse*, its muskets still neatly stacked. It was the most serious crisis of the battle for Lee. If Meade could be reinforced, Longstreet and Jackson's commands could be split in two and defeated in detail. The deployment of another corps into the gap created by Meade could probably have rolled up Longstreet's flank, clearing Marye's Heights, and turned the tide of battle. In fact

Above: A *Confederate artilleryman's haversack.*

Burnside had a whole "grand division" under Hooker stationed on the north bank of the Rappahannock River, but it did nothing throughout the day apart from use its artillery to support Sumner's doomed advance.

Jackson reacted with characteristic efficiency, sending Early's Division over from his right flank to plug the gap in his left. To win a breathing space A.P. Hill launched a counterattack on Meade's left, but his Confederate brigade were committed piecemeal and were outnumbered by the Union troops on the slopes of Prospect Hill. As a result the Confederates suffered badly before Early's men arrived and launched a better co-ordinated counterattack against nearby brigades besides Meade's lodgment. Unsupported and under increasing pressure, Meade and Gibbons were forced to withdraw, and Lee's right flank was secure. The crisis was over. A brief attempt was made at a Confederate

Below: *The stone wall in front of Marye's Heights served to anchor the Confederate line.*

pursuit, but this ended when Early's men ran into a firing line formed by the rest of Franklin's command. This was the sole contribution to the battle made by these troops. Apart from that, Franklin did nothing with the 20,000 men in the other four divisions he commanded, and his "grand division" spent the rest of the afternoon lined up along the Old Richmond Road, well out of musket range of the Confederates on Prospect Hill.

Meanwhile the suicidal Union assault on Marye's Heights continued as Burnside ordered a third and final attack spearheaded by Brigadier-General Butterfield's veteran V

Above: *The advance of Humphrey's Division at Fredericksburg.*

Far right: *The commemorative statue on Marye's Heights to Richard Kirkland, Company G, 2d South Carolina Volunteers, CSA. Known as "The Angel of Marye's Heights," Rowland risked his own life to take water to the dying and wounded of both sides in no-man's land in the aftermath of the assault.*

Corps from Hooker's "grand division," hoping to relieve the pressure on the broken troops of Sumner's command. As Kershaw's Brigade had reinforced the Confederates behind the stone wall, the fire from Marye's Heights was even more devastating than before, and Butterfield's men were repulsed with heavy losses. As darkness fell Burnside finally decided the battle was lost, and he called off any further attacks. In one bloody day's fighting, over 12,500 Union troops had fallen, 10,000 of whom had done so in front of Marye's Heights. By contrast Lee's army had lost a little under 5,000 men killed or wounded, the majority of the casualties being sustained by Jackson's Corps. Accurately assessing the results of the battle, a Union newspaper correspondent wrote; "It can hardly be in human nature from men to show more valor, or generals to manifest less judgment." This reflected the common reaction to the slaughter by the North. Burnside's days in command were numbered—but he had one more card to play.

Two weeks after the battle he led his army away from Fredericksburg in an attempt to outflank Lee, and cross the Rappahannock River further upstream. Although the operation began well enough, heavy rain made the roads all but impassable, and after 24 hours Burnside gave up and returned to his camp opposite Fredericksburg. This "mud march" proved to be the last straw, and deprived him of any remaining authority he enjoyed. On January 25th Lincoln removed him from his command, replacing him with Major-General "Fighting Joe" Hooker. Fredericksburg had given Lee his easiest victory, and witnessed one of the most spectacularly unsuccessful assaults of the war.

Chancellorsville
May 2–3, 1863

Chancellorsville has become known as "Lee's greatest victory." Major-General Joseph Hooker, who replaced Burnside following the Fredericksburg debacle, moved to oust Lee from his Fredericksburg entrenchments, and the two sides came to battle at Chancellorsville. Among those killed was "Stonewall" Jackson. Today the site is preserved as part of the Fredericksburg and Spotsylvania National Military Park, with the Chancellorsville Battlefield Visitor Center located 12 miles west of Fredericksburg.

Right: *Troops of Joseph Hooker's army (Brook's Division of Sedgwick's Sixth Corps) entrenched along the banks of the Rappahannock River in May 1863.*

Below: *The detritus of war: the dead and debris at the stonewall, Marye's Heights, Fredericksburg, which saw continued fighting during the battle of Chancellorsville.*

When Major-General Joseph "Fighting Joe" Hooker took command of the Army of the Potomac in late-January 1863 he was determined to avoid the mistakes made by his predecessor. While working to rebuild the morale of the army, he examined ways to outmaneuver the Confederates and to successfully establish his army on the southern bank of the Rappahannock River. He also worked hard throughout the winter and spring to improve his intelligence network, which gave the army a better understanding of where Lee's army was, and how many troops he had at his disposal.

Hooker also reorganized the Union cavalry, which he considered the weakest part of his army, and incapable of performing its vital task of screening the army on the march. Meanwhile the army remained inactive, allowing Lee to send Longstreet and 10,000 troops south to counter Union attacks in the Carolinas. Although Lee was now outnumbered by two-to-one, he felt that his strong defensive position at Fredericksburg more than compensated for this deficiency. However, Hooker had little intention of launching a frontal attack as Burnside had done. Instead he planned a wide flanking maneuver that would involve the bulk of his army, leaving just two corps behind at Fredericksburg to oppose Lee. Hooker began his offensive on April 26th, sending his cavalry under the command of Brigadier-General Stoneman across the Rappahannock River a few miles upstream of Fredericksburg, to disrupt Confederate communications with Richmond. The rest of the army followed on behind.

He sent three corps from his army on a circuitous route to Kelly's Ford, some 20 miles upriver from the army's winter camp at Falmouth. Two other corps were also ordered to prepare to march, while the corps of major-generals Sedgwick (VI Corps) and Reynolds (I Corps) remained at Fredericksburg, on the north bank facing the city. When the Union columns had been sent on their way, Hooker ordered his two remaining corps, commanded by major-generals Couch (II Corps) and Sickles (III Corps), to march west along the north bank of the Rappahannock River for nine miles to the U.S. Ford, where another bridgehead would be established. Meanwhile the corps of major-generals Meade (V Corps), Howard (XI Corps) and Slocum (XII Corps) had crossed the Rappahannock at Kelly's Ford, and had turned

Following pages: *Hooker's crossing of the Rappahannock took Lee by surprise. As his forces advanced into The Wilderness, Hooker planned for Sedgwick, facing Fredericksburg, to make a demonstration and hold the bulk of Lee's forces there, while Hooker moved against Lee's rear via the Orange Turnpike. Sedgwick failed to act with alacrity, allowing Lee to advance to meet Hooker's threat. On May 1st Hooker took Chancellorsville, while Lee sent Jackson with several divisions on a sweeping flank march via the Brock Road to attack Howard's flank and rear. On May 2nd, Jackson drove into the Federal troops, causing mayhem. The next day Hooker struggled to hold his position at Chancellorsville, and concentrated on saving his army. On May 3–4 at Fredericksburg Sedgwick launched a more spirited attack, but by now Lee had reinforced the lines, and Hooker eventually withdrew.*

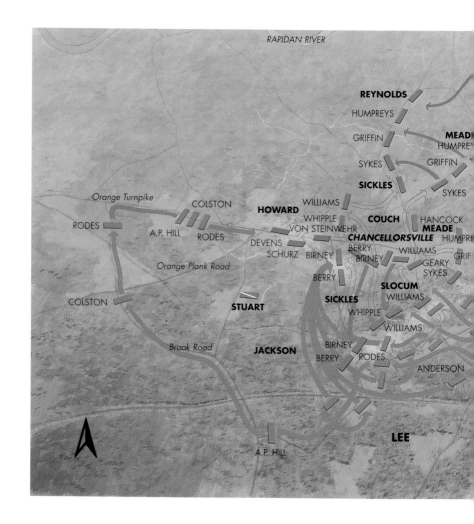

RAPIDAN RIVER

REYNOLDS

HUMPREYS

GRIFFIN

MEAD
HUMPRE

SYKES

GRIFFIN

SICKLES

SYKES

Orange Turnpike

COLSTON

WILLIAMS

HOWARD

WHIPPLE

COUCH

HANCOCK
MEADE

RODES

VON STEINWEHR

CHANCELLORSVILLE

HUMPRI

A.P. HILL

RODES

DEVENS

SCHURZ

BIRNEY

BERRY

WILLIAMS

GRIF

Orange Plank Road

BIRNEY

GEARY

SYKES

BERRY

SLOCUM

COLSTON

SICKLES

WILLIAMS

STUART

WHIPPLE

WILLIAMS

Brook Road

BIRNEY

JACKSON

BERRY

RODES

ANDERSON

LEE

A.P. HILL

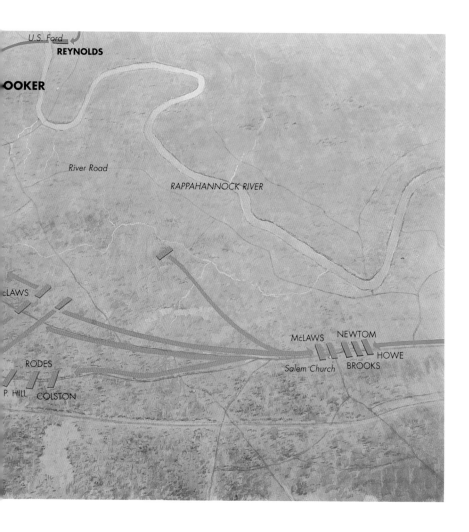

U.S. Ford
REYNOLDS

OOKER

River Road

RAPPAHANNOCK RIVER

cLAWS

McLAWS   NEWTOM

Salem Church   HOWE
BROOKS

RODES

P. HILL   COLSTON

south to cross the Rapidan River in two columns. V Corps crossed at Ely's Ford while Howard and Slocum used the Germanna Ford. All these fords were unguarded, save by Confederate cavalry patrols, so no serious opposition was encountered during the operation. These three columns rendezvous-ed at the little crossroads of Chancellorsville, some four miles south of the confluence of the Rappahannock and Rapidan rivers, and the site of a large brick house named after the family who lived there. Meanwhile the engineers of I Corps and VI Corps built pontoon bridges, allowing Sedgwick and Slocum to re-occupy Fredericksburg, and deploy facing the Confederate positions on Marye's Heights.

This all meant that by the evening of May 30th, five out of seven corps in the Army of the Potomac, a total of 83,000 men, had successfully crossed the river barrier, and were concentrated on Lee's left flank less than ten miles west of Fredericksburg. Two more corps were also lodged on the

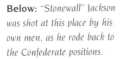

Below: *"Stonewall" Jackson was shot at this place by his own men, as he rode back to the Confederate positions.*

THOMAS J. JACKSON (1824–63)

Next to Lee and possibly Grant, "Stonewall" Jackson is the best-remembered general of the war. The Virginian-born general was educated at West Point and fought in Mexico, before becoming a lecturer at the Virginia Military Academy. Soon after the war began, he was given command of a brigade, and his performance at 1st Manassas earned him his nickname—a name shared by his brigade, which came to be regarded as the elite formation in the army. He returned to the Shenandoah to defend it against a series of Union attacks, and his handling of the campaign was nothing short of brilliant. He held the valley against superior forces, and defeated each enemy force in detail during the summer of 1862, winning victories at Front Royal, Winchester, Cross Keys and Port Republic. By this time his brigade had become a small army, and "Stonewall's Army of the Shenandoah" was next called upon to defend Richmond during Lee's Seven Days' Campaign. Jackson's performance was lacklustre during this period, a failure probably due to chronic fatigue. The following month he was back to his usual form, defeating elements of Pope's army at Cedar Mountain, then playing a major part in Lee's victory at 2nd Manassas. By this time Jackson had become an invaluable deputy to Lee, fighting alongside him at Antietam, Fredericksburg and Chickamauga. In his last battle Jackson led the majority of Lee's army in a daring attack, winning Lee his greatest victory. It also cost Jackson his life. Wounded in the arm, he died several days later following complications caused by its amputation. Lee had lost a valued commander.

south side of the river, waiting for the chance to expand their bridgehead if Lee moved his army off the Heights that dominated the town. So far the operation had proved a stunning success, and the Confederate army had been outmaneuvered, and left in an extremely dangerous position. A dense forest with tangled, almost impenetrable undergrowth filled the area around Chancellorsville, giving the area the somewhat melancholy name of "The Wilderness." Hooker believed the thick woods would mask his outflanking maneuver for a few days, until he was ready to attack Lee's left flank. However, Lee was well aware of Hooker's presence at Chancellorsville, having been kept abreast of Union movements by J.E.B. Stuart's cavalry. Lee had several options. He could launch an attack against the Union troops still at Fredericksburg; he could split his army to fight both forces; or he could move west to confront Hooker's main force at Chancellorsville. Of the three options, this last carried the greatest risk of failure, but Lee realized that in order to maintain his moral ascendancy over the Army of the Potomac, he had to find a way to drive Hooker back over the Rappahannock River. He opted to march west.

Hooker spent the morning of May 1st preparing his army for the coming assault on Fredericksburg, bringing up supplies and resting his men. It was not until the afternoon that he formed his army into two columns and began his advance down the Orange Plank Road and the Orange Turnpike, two routes that converged a few miles beyond the Wilderness at Salem Church. However, the leading troops in both columns were still within the confines of the forest when they ran into Confederate skirmish lines, and the advance was halted. These were the advance elements of

Lee's army. Although Hooker still had the benefit of superior numbers, he halted the advance, then ordered his men to pull back to Chancellorsville, where they formed a defensive position and awaited Lee's attack. This was a major error, as by pressing on Hooker's men would have reached the open terrain beyond the Wilderness, where their superiority in numbers and in artillery would have had the most pronounced effect on the outcome of the forthcoming battle. By withdrawing, Hooker was also surrendering the initiative to Lee.

Lee then threw the book of military theory away, and divided his army in two, sending Jackson with some 25,000

Below: *Men of the Federal Irish Brigade (2nd Brigade of the 1st Division, 2nd Army Corps.) The brigade fought at Antietam, Fredericksburg, Chancellorsvile and Gettysburg.*

men on a long, circuitous flanking march around Hooker's Army. It would then attack from the west. This was probably the most audacious decision made by Lee during the entire war, as it involved marching the bulk of his army across the front of a superior force. It also meant that Lee was left with just 15,000 men to face Hooker.

Jackson began his march at 10am on May 2nd, leaving Lee at a point south of Chancellorsville, then heading west for three miles to Catherine's Furnace. At this point he was within sight of Union outposts, but the majority of Jackson's command managed to pass this dangers spot without being detected. When a skirmish erupted between Union patrols and Jackson's rearguard, Hooker assumed that the Confederates his men reported to be marching to the south were part of Lee's army, which must have been in retreat.

Shortly after 3pm Jackson's advance units crossed the Orange Plank Road, which led onto the flank of Howard's XI Corps. He considered attacking up the road, but decided to press on to the north, as an attack launched from the Orange Turnpike would emerge behind Howard's flank, and would therefore be more decisive. By 5pm his troops were deployed along the turnpike, close to the Union troops encamped around Wilderness Church. The Union soldiers were cooking dinner, and were startled to find themselves

under attack from such an unexpected quarter. The Confederate battleline swept over them before they had time to form up. As the men of Howard's Corps were routed, the panic threatened to spread throughout the rest of the army. Jackson, urging his men on with cries of "Press them! Press them!", realized that victory was dependent on preventing the defenders from recovering from the surprise assault. This attack placed Hooker in a difficult position, as his army was deployed facing Lee, and he struggled to redeploy his troops to face the new threat. However, the Confederates were delayed by the terrain, and by the temptations offered by the abandoned Union encampments. This gave Hooker the chance to pull back parts of III Corps and XII Corps to form an improvised defensive line. The fighting continued after sunset (shortly before 7pm) but the chance of a decisive victory appeared to be slipping away from Jackson. He rode ahead of his army with his staff, scouting a track that led to the northeast, and offered him the chance to cut off the Union pocket around Chancellorsville. As he returned from this reconnaissance foray, Confederate pickets fired on what they presumed was a group of enemy horsemen approaching them through the woods. Jackson was hit twice once in the left arm, and once in the right hand. Although the wounds were debilitating,

Above: The 0.58-caliber J.P Murray cavalry carbine. This gun was produced in Columbus, Georgia. Many different types of carbine were manufactured during the course of the war. Among the most famous and popular examples were the Sharps rifle and the Spencer carbine.

they did not appear to be life-threatening. Jackson was taken to the rear and the command of his corps devolved to Major-General A.P. Hill; when he was wounded shortly afterwards, command of the flanking force went to J.E.B. Stuart. By this time night had fallen, and the drive to cut off the Union army around Chancellorsville ended. Lee and Stuart would have to wait until dawn to see if they could resume their offensive, but their troops were still separated by Hooker's army.

During the night Hooker ordered Sedgwick to break through the Confederate defenses at Fredericksburg and march to his aid, while Reynolds was ordered up to the U.S.

Ford. Stuart resumed his attack at dawn, driving the Union defenders back towards Chancellorsville. Lee also attacked, and at 10am the two Confederate forces were reunited. Hooker was lightly wounded, and Major-General Couch assumed temporary command of the army. He ordered a withdrawal to the north, and at noon Lee rode up to the Chancellor House, to the cheers of his men who realized they were on the verge of victory. Couch established a new defensive line two miles to the north, stretched between the Rapidan and Rappahannock rivers, covering the U.S. Ford.

Lee then learned that Sedgwick's VI Corps had brushed aside the Confederate division of Jubal Early on Marye's Heights, and was now approaching Chancellorsville along the Turnpike. Lee sent McClaws' Divison ahead to delay VI Corps, planning to follow with reinforcements. The Confederates held Sedgwick at Salem Church, and the following day (May 4th) Lee left Stuart to contain Couch, then marched to deal with Sedgwick's 20,000 men, now with their backs to the river. It was 6pm before he was in a position to attack, but VI Corps held on until dark, when they withdrew back over the Rappahannock via U.S Ford. Hooker did the same, and by dawn the dispirited Army of the Potomac was back on the north bank of the river.

Lee had won his greatest victory, defeating an army twice his size through spirited generalship. The battle cost Hooker 16,800 men killed and wounded, while Lee lost around 10,000 men. However, the most significant casualty was "Stonewall Jackson", who died of an infection following the amputation of his arm after the battle. It was a great loss to the Confederate cause, but the victory Jackson helped win gave Lee the chance to go onto the offensive, and take the war to the enemy.

Gettysburg
July 1–3, 1863

Lee's second invasion of the North was something of a gamble. He hoped to force Lincoln into negotiations, and gain the support of the European powers. Following the setbacks of Fredericksburg and Chancellorsville, Meade's Army of the Potomac needed to prove itself. Gettysburg marked the "high-water mark" of the Confederacy, and was the largest battle of the war. Today the Gettysburg National Military Park, located 50 miles northwest of Baltimore, PA, comprises nearly 6,000 acres, and contains the Soldiers' National Cemetery.

Right: *The Pennsylvania Monument, Gettysburg. On the base of monument is a plaque dedicated to each of the Pennsylvania regiments that fought there.*

In late-May Longstreet returned to the army, his two divisions increasing Lee's strength to just over 70,000 men. Following the death of "Stonewall" Jackson, Lee reorganized his army into three groups: 1st Corps, commanded by Major-General Longstreet; 2nd Corps, commanded by Major-General Richard Ewell; and 3rd Corps, commanded by Major-General A.P. Hill. He also moved his base of operations from Fredericksburg to Paul Pepper on the Orange and Alexandria Railroad where he was able to threaten Hooker's army, which had withdrawn to Manassas. J.E.B. Stuart's cavalry division now consisted of 10,000 men—a force which would be able to screen any movement of the army. On June 7th Lee inspected Stuart's cavalry at a grand review held at Brandy Station. On hearing of this, the Union cavalry commander Major-General Pleasanton took 11,000 troopers of his own down the railroad line to Brandy Station, and attacked Stuart on June 9th. At first Stuart's men were hard pressed, but eventually a Confederate charge drove the Union horsemen from the field; after Lee's approach with infantry reinforcements, Pleasanton withdrew. It was the largest cavalry battle of the war, and Stuart felt aggrieved that he let himself be taken by surprise—something that may have led to him being "over-zealous" in the weeks that followed.

With the Union army temporarily cowed, Lee decided to move to the offensive, launching a second invasion of the North in an attempt to take the seat of fighting away from Virginia. By securing a decisive victory on northern soil Lee hoped to force a conclusion to the war. Ewell's Corps led the advance into the Shenandoah Valley, crushing a Union division at Winchester on June 14th then advancing towards the Potomac River. Longstreet and A.P. Hill followed behind

him with their corps, crossing the Potomac opposite Sharpsburg, then striking north towards Hagerstown and into Pennsylvania. Meanwhile, on June 25th J.E.B. Stuart led his cavalry force around Manassas, bypassed Hooker's army, then crossed the Potomac into Maryland.

When Hooker heard of Lee's offensive, he proposed an offensive of his own against Richmond, but President Lincoln overruled him, stressing that "Lee's army, and not Richmond, is your true objective." The Army of the Potomac duly marched north to intercept Lee somewhere beyond the Potomac. This exposed the Union garrison at Harper's Ferry,

Above: *The fighting in the Devil's Den was fierce. Many bodies were left where they fell, amid the jumble of boulders and rocks.*

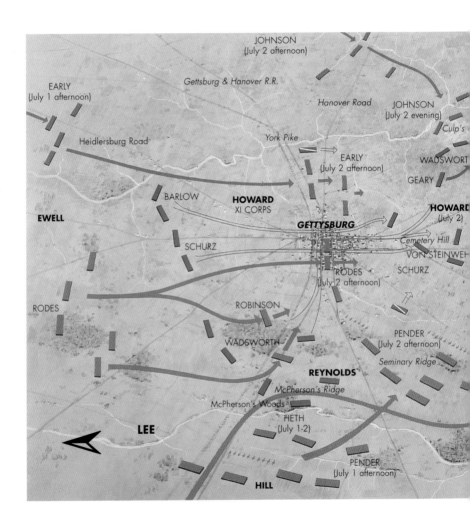

JOHNSON
(July 2 afternoon)

EARLY
(July 1 afternoon)

Gettsburg & Hanover R.R.

Hanover Road

JOHNSON
(July 2 evening)

Culp's

Heidlersburg Road

York Pike

EARLY
(July 2 afternoon)

WADSWORT

GEARY

BARLOW

HOWARD
XI CORPS

EWELL

GETTYSBURG

HOWARD
(July 2)

SCHURZ

Cemetery Hill

VON STEINWEH

RODES
(July 2 afternoon)

SCHURZ

RODES

ROBINSON

PENDER
(July 2 afternoon)

WADSWORTH

Seminary Ridge

REYNOLDS

McPherson's Ridge

McPherson's Woods

HETH
(July 1-2)

LEE

PENDER
(July 1 afternoon)

HILL

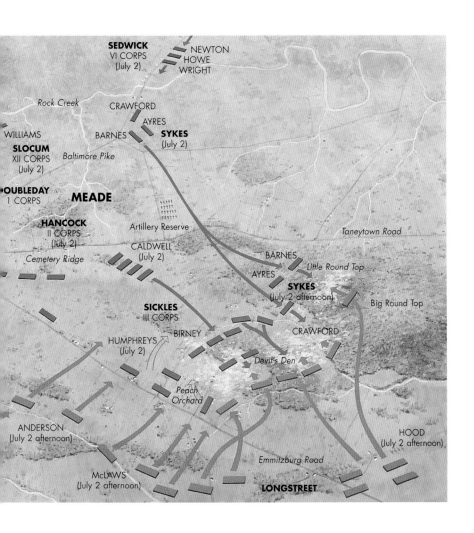

SEDWICK
VI CORPS
(July 2)

NEWTON
HOWE
WRIGHT

Rock Creek

CRAWFORD

AYRES

BARNES

SYKES
(July 2)

WILLIAMS

SLOCUM
XII CORPS
(July 2)

Baltimore Pike

OUBLEDAY
1 CORPS

MEADE

HANCOCK
II CORPS
(July 2)

Cemetery Ridge

Artillery Reserve

CALDWELL
(July 2)

BARNES

AYRES

Taneytown Road

Little Round Top

SYKES
(July 2 afternoon)

Big Round Top

SICKLES
III CORPS

HUMPHREYS
(July 2)

BIRNEY

CRAWFORD

Devil's Den

Peach
Orchard

ANDERSON
(July 2 afternoon)

McLAWS
(July 2 afternoon)

Emmitzburg Road

LONGSTREET

HOOD
(July 2 afternoon)

Previous pages: *The first two days at Gettysburg form an interesting study in the gradual development of a major battle. Early on July 1st, advance elements of the Army of the Potomac entered the town from the south, to find A.P. Hill's Confederates approaching from the north and northwest. Here the battle rapidly developed as more troops gravitated towards the sound of the guns. The fighting north of the town was furious; Reynolds fell in action, and the Federals were finally pushed back to Cemetery Hill, where Hancock took over. Reinforcements arrived during the night, and reconnaissance and reorganization took place. The fighting began again in late-afternoon the next day, when Longstreet attacked Meade's left and Little Round Top. In the Peach Orchard, Sickle's III Corps was almost destroyed. The Confederate assaults on Little Round Top, Cemetery Hill and Culp's Hill all failed to break through.*

a move which led to a robust exchange between Hooker, Halleck and Lincoln. When Hooker stood his ground and offered to resign over the issue, Lincoln accepted, appointing Major-General George Meade as commander in his place on June 28th. At this point the Army of the Potomac was at Frederick, Marlyand, while Stuart was between the Union army and Washington, disrupting Meade's supply lines. Ewell (supported by Early's Division) was advancing deep into Pennsylvania, reaching Carlisle, while Early pushed on to the Susquehanna River. On June 28th Lee was with Hill and Longstreet near Chambersburg, Pennsylvania, when he learned that the Army of the Potomac was now at Frederick, just 40 miles to the south. He responded by recalling his scattered columns, ordering them to concentrate around the little town of Gettysburg, Pennsylvania.

On June 30th a Union cavalry division commanded by Major-General Buford entered Gettysburg from the south. Knowing that the Confederates were close by, he moved through the town and set up a defensive line along McPherson's Ridge, immediately to the west. His troops now lay between the corps of Longstreet and A.P. Hill approaching from the west and that of Early, moving down from the north. Heth's Division (part of Hill's Corps) was the first Confederate formation to arrive, and launched an attack shortly after 8am the following morning (July 1st). The dismounted cavalrymen were armed with repeating carbines, and were able to hold off the attackers until noon when Union reinforcements (Major-General Reynold's I Corps, which was force-marching up from the south) arrived. Other units of Hill's Corps also appeared, and were fed into the fighting. Although Reynolds was killed within minutes of reaching the battlefield, his troops forced the Confederates to pull back, giving Buford's cavalry some respite. Lee arrived at 2pm, and Ewell's Corps began to arrive on the Union right flank. Seizing the opportunity, Lee ordered a general advance. Brigadier-General Doubleday, now commanding I Corps, pulled his men back in the face of enemy attacks, lining his flank up with Howard's XI Corps, which had just deployed to the north of Gettysburg. Ewell ordered Rhodes' Divison into the attack, and just as they had done at Chancellorsville, and Howard's men broke and ran. This forced Doubleday and Buford to pull back as well, retreating through the town to Seminary Ridge, which lay beyond it to the south.

The Confederates pursued them through Gettysburg, and as dusk fell it was clear that the Confederates had won the first round. If Ewell had continued his pursuit he might well have captured the high ground before nightfall, but mindful of Lee's instructions not to bring on a full-scale battle before the army had concentrated, he halted his men. The opportunity soon passed as Hancock's II Corps arrived, and deployed along the ridge, and on Culp's Hill to the right. The Union troops held this ridge, and reinforcements were brought up through the night, but the Confederates were grouped around in a large semicircle, and would certainly launch a full-scale attack the following day. The stage was set for the great battle that would decide the course of the war.

On July 2nd, four Union corps (II, III, XI and XII) and

Above: *Cemetery Hill, Gettysburg. In the afternoon of the first day, having been driven back through town, in the confusion thousands of Union soldiers were captured before they could rally on Cemetery Hill, south of town.*

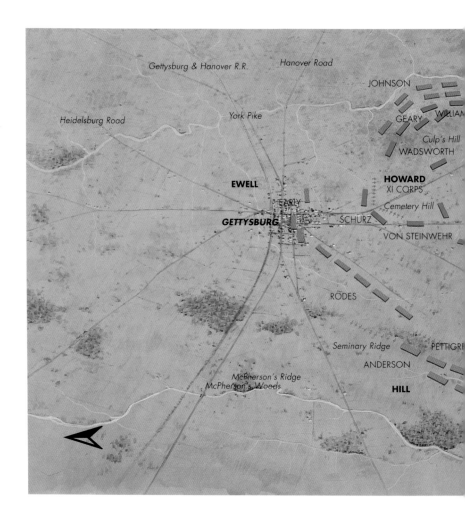

Gettysburg & Hanover R.R.

Hanover Road

JOHNSON

Heidelsburg Road

York Pike

GEARY WILLIAM

Culp's Hill
WADSWORTH

EWELL

HOWARD
XI CORPS

EARLY

Cemetery Hill

GETTYSBURG

SCHURZ

VON STEINWEHR

RÖDES

Seminary Ridge PETTIGRE

ANDERSON

McPherson's Ridge
McPherson's Woods

HILL

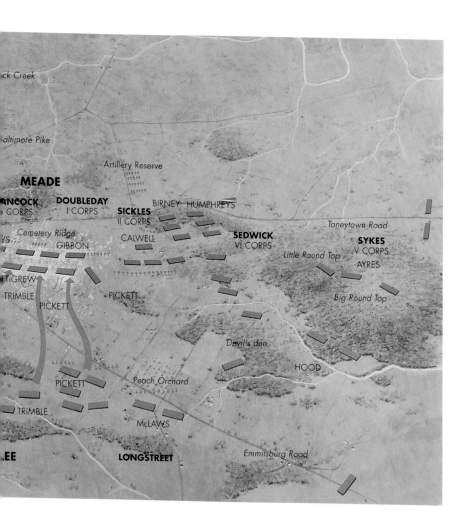

ck Creek

altimore Pike

Artillery Reserve

MEADE

NCOCK | **DOUBLEDAY** | BIRNEY HUMPHREYS
CORPS | I CORPS | **SICKLES**
| | II CORPS | Taneytown Road

Cemetery Ridge | CALWELL | **SEDWICK** | **SYKES**
YS | GIBBON | | VI CORPS | V CORPS
| | | Little Round Top | AYRES

TIGREW

TRIMBLE | PICKETT
PICKETT | | Big Round Top

Devil's den

PICKETT | | HOOD

TRIMBLE | | Peach Orchard

McLAWS

EE | **LONGSTREET** | Emmitsburg Road

Previous pages: *During the night of July 2nd, Lee and Meade prepared their armies for what was to come. Meade anticipated an attack in his center, and Lee concentrated his artillery to fire against this area. On July 3rd, Lee's artillery assault was largely ineffective, overshooting the target, and when the 15,000-strong attack of Picket and Pettigrew advanced the Federal artillery was still in place. After a march across one mile of open ground, the Confederates were met by a hail of artillery and smallshot fire. Rushing up the rocky slope of the Union position, the two sides met face to face, and the combat was vicious—often hand to hand. The Federal I and II Corps held their ground, with only portions of Armistead's and Garnett's brigades penetrating the lines. The Confederate tide withdrew towards Seminary Ridge, the assault ending in failure. Other Confederate moves by Ewell and Stuart also failed.*

elements of two others (I and V) were deployed in a "fishhook" running from Culp's Hill and Cemetery Hill in the north, then along Cemetery Ridge to Little Round Top some two miles south of Gettysburg itself. By noon Meade would have six full corps at his disposal, together with the army's Reserve Artillery, while Sedgwick's VI Corps would arrive in mid-afternoon. He had parity of numbers with Lee at dawn, and a superiority in manpower as the day wore on. His dispositions were good, his troops holding an interior line of high ground, although Major-General Sickles commanding III Corps had moved his troops forward slightly to occupy a more readily defensible line along the Emmitsburg Road. This created a gap between his right flank and the left flank of Hancock's II Corps on Cemetery Ridge. On Sickles' left flank the dominating high ground of Little Round Top remained unoccupied by anyone other than signalmen, and Longstreet noticed this when he deployed his troops to attack Sickles' position. By holding Little Round Top Longstreet could outflank Sickles, and sever the road that lay beyond the hill, cutting Meade's army off from the south.

Lee held his men in check throughout the morning while Longstreet's Corps arrived, and deployed to the south of A.P. Hill's Corps on Missionary Ridge, a crest running parallel to Cemetery Ridge, just over a mile to the west. Longstreet was finally ready to attack at 2pm, but he spent the next two hours marching and counter-marching his units in an attempt to conceal the direction of his attack from the enemy. It was 4pm when he launched his attack on III Corps, Hood's Division on his right flank advancing on Little Round Top and the gully in front of it known as the Devil's Den. It was at this stage that Meades's staff informed him that Little

ROBERT E. LEE (1807–70)

Robert E. Lee was the son of "Light Horse" Harry Lee, a Virginian hero of the American Revolution. The young Lee was brought up in a tradition of military service. After graduating from West Point he joined the US Engineers, spending the early part of his career supervising the construction of coastal fortifications. He fought with distinction in the Mexican-American War, and then became the Superintendent of West Point. In 1859 he quelled the John Brown Rebellion at Harper's Ferry, and when the war broke out he was offered overall command of the Union army. He turned this down and resigned his commission, preferring to serve Virginia rather than participate in the invasion of his beloved home state. President Davis accepted Lee into the Confederate Army in May 1861, appointing him as the President's military advisor the following spring. Following General Johnston's wounding at the Battle of Fair Oaks, Lee assumed command of the Confederate Army in front of Richmond, a body he renamed "The Army of Northern Virginia." The fate of Lee and this army would become intertwined, and he led these men to victory in several key battles before his defeat at Gettysburg in July 1863. After Gettysburg, Lee was on the defensive, with his army steadily pushed back to Petersburg during 1864. His command ended with the surrender of his army at Appomattox Courthouse in April 1865. Much has been written about Lee, and although many revisionist historians have criticized him, the Virginian still remains as one of the great commanders of history. His quiet, calm manner inspired his men with confidence, and fostered their loyalty.

Below: *Union soldiers of the 107th US Colored Regiment, organized at Louisville, Kentucky. These troops have bayonets fixed to their rifles. For most Confederate and Federal troops, the fighting at Gettysburg was the first and only time that hand-to-hand combat was experienced.*

Round Top was undefended, so he ordered Major-General Sykes of V Corps to send two brigades and some artillery to seize and hold the position. They arrived just as the Confederates were approaching the summit and a vicious battle followed for control of the hill; the summit changed hands several times throughout the afternoon. While this was taking place Sickles' Corps was under heavy attack from McClaws' Division of Longstreet's Corps. The Union line extended through a peach orchard and a wheatfield and both features became arenas for some bloody, close-quarter fighting as III Corps was driven from one feature to the other.

Sickles' line was slowly pushed back, but Confederate casualties were high, and it looked as if III Corps might hold out. Then, late in the afternoon, McClaws found a gap in the Union line near the wheatfield and concentrated his efforts there. The Union line finally broke, and Longstreet ordered McClaws to continue the attack across the creek known as Plum Run. By this stage the attackers were exhausted, and the assault ground to a halt along the creek, below the slope of Cemetery Ridge, where concentrated Union artillery fire and the reinforcements of Major-General Slocum's XII Corps convinced Longstreet his attack would not succeed. These Union reinforcements saved the right flank of the Army of the Potomac by plugging the gap on Howard's left flank and finally securing Little Round Top. By dusk Hood was forced to concede defeat and withdraw his men back over Devil's Den.

Lee had planned to launch a rolling attack that would sweep from right to left along Cemetery Ridge. When Longstreet was fully engaged, he ordered A.P. Hill to send Anderson's Division against the southern portion of Cemetery Ridge, where the gap was located between II Corps and III Corps. The attackers actually veered a little to the left, hitting Hancock's line directly. One of Anderson's brigades actually crested the top of the ridge, and for a moment it looked as if Anderson was going to roll up Hancock's flank.

Reinforcements were thrown into the fighting, and a new Union line was established a short distance to the rear. It held, and as fresh Union reinforcements arrived, Anderson ordered his men to retire. The attack had been driven off, as had the diversionary attacks launched on Cemetery Hill and Culp's Hill by Early and Johnson's divisions of Ewell's

Corps. At one point the Confederates actually held Culp's Hill, driving the men of Slocum's XII Corps back onto the eastern side of Cemetery Hill, but as night fell the Union line remained battered but intact all along the line. The Confederates had fought hard but they had failed to achieve a breakthrough. Union reinforcements were still arriving, and by the following day Lee would be outnumbered by three-to-two. The Army of Northern Virginia would have to rely on its *élan* rather than its numbers to win the battle the following day.

Meade met with his corps commanders on the evening of July 2nd, and it was decided to continue to fight a defensive battle. He fully expected Lee to launch another attack, and after the attacks on his left and right flanks the previous day, Meade expected the assault to come in his center. However, Lee planned to launch a large, co-ordinated attack along his entire front, starting from his left where Johnson's Division was already deployed on the lower slopes of Culp's Hill, down the line to Hood's Division at Devil's Den, now commanded by Brigadier-General Law. He then changed his mind, as reports from Law and Longstreet indicated how exhausted their troops really were. Instead Lee elected to launch a large assault on the right of the union center, a position held by Hancock's II Corps. This would involve 15,000 men from three divisions; Pickett's Division from Longstreet's Corps, which had arrived on the battlefield the previous evening; and the divisions of Heth and Pender from A.P. Hill's Corps.

An artillery duel lasted for two hours, but the Confederate gunners were unable to silence the Union batteries on Cemetery Ridge. Just after 3pm Lee gave the order to advance. Between the Confederate starting positions on

Seminary Ridge and the Union line on Cemetery Ridge lay a mile of open ground. Pickett called on his men to "honor Virginia," and aimed his troops towards a clump of trees on the ridge that marked the center of Hancock's position. This brought them veering over to the left, causing the attackers to bunch up as they advanced, and it soon appeared that all 15,000 men were heading towards the same spot. As they advanced, artillery shells began to burst amongst the ranks, while enfilading fire from Cemetery Hill and Little Round Top began ripping through the lines of troops. By the time

Far right: *National Guidon of Company C, 3rd Pennsylvania Cavalry, issued at the close of the war and carried by that unit in the Grand Review of the Army of the Potomac along Pennsylvania Avenue, Washington DC, on May 23, 1865. Gettysburg is one of the many battle honors cited by this unit in gilt paint on the flag.*

the attackers reached the Emmitsburg Road they were within canister range, and great gaps appeared in the Confederate ranks. The advance continued through this hail of fire, until the leading ranks reached the low stone wall that marked the front of Hancock's line. The Confederates charged, the assault spearheaded by Brigadier-General Armistead of Pickett's Division, who led his men with his hat held high on the tip of his sword. His men reached the line of Union guns, but they were the only Confederates to reach that far, the rest being stopped at or on the stone wall. Unsupported and heavily outnumbered, Armistead's men were soon killed, captured or driven back, and the attack failed. The remnants of "Pickett's Charge" began to make their way back across the valley, leaving almost half their number dead or wounded behind them. The casualties included Armistead, who was killed just beyond the Union guns, his body marking the high-water mark of Confederate fortunes for that day, and for the whole of the war.

A heartbroken Lee rode out to meet the survivors as they straggled back onto Seminary Ridge, and was heard to exclaim: "Too bad ... oh, too bad!". Any further attacks were out of the question, as it was clear Lee's army was in no shape to continue the fight. Meade remained on the defensive, and that night, under the cover of heavy rain, the defeated Army of Northern Virginia left that awful, blood-soaked, Pennsylvania valley, and made their way back to Virginia. Meade had won a great defensive victory, and President Lincoln was delighted, realizing Gettysburg marked a true turning point in the war. Four months later he chose the battlefield as the venue for his "Gettysburg Address," a speech given at the commemoration of a cemetery to the Union dead, which effectively elevated the

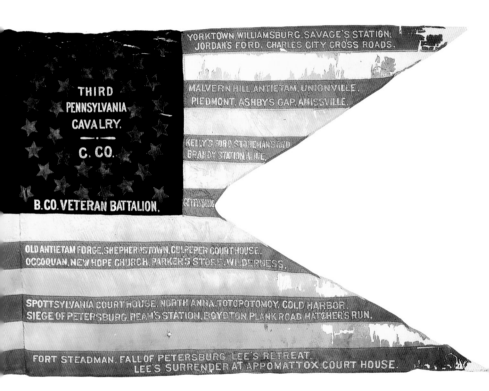

Union cause to something akin to a crusade. Before, Union troops were fighting to forcibly restore an unpopular union at the expense of the rights of individual states to determine their own affairs. After Gettysburg, they were fighting for the greater moral good.

The Wilderness & Spotsylvania
May 4–20, 1864

The spring campaign of 1864 saw much bloody fighting. The Battle of the Wilderness gave Lee a tactical victory, though the losses incurred here and at Spotsylvania Court House would prove too great to bear. The Army of the Potomac, now under Ulysses S. Grant, also suffered greatly, but was better resourced. The battlefields now form part of the Fredericksburg and Spotsylvania National Military Park, centered around Fredericksburg, VA. Among the sites preserved are Ellwood Manor, Todd's Tavern, and the Bloody Angle.

Right: *The Battle of the Wilderness; Grant pressed forward, but exhaustion on both sides would deny either a decisive victory.*

After Gettysburg, Lee retreated back into central Virginia, taking up his old defensive positions near Culpeper, behind the Rappahannock River. His army had been reduced to just 60,000 men, while Meades's Army of the Potomac had double Lee's strength. For Lee the winter of 1863/64 was a hard one, as his army was now short of supplies, equipment and above all, recruits. On March 8, 1864 Lincoln appointed Lieutenant-General Ulysses S. Grant as overall commander of all Union forces. The President had no specific orders for his new commander, so was delighted when Grant defined his strategy as "going after Lee." This was a general with a tradition of victory, a great improvement over those who had preceded him. While Meade retained control of the Army of the Potomac, rather than await events in Washington, Grant attached his headquarters to the Army of the Potomac in the field, and remained with his troops for the duration of the war. Clearly Grant felt that he could leave the war in the West in Sherman's capable hands.

Right: *Men of the 44th New York Regiment, who fought at the Wilderness. They camped near Alexandria, Virginia for an extended period early in 1864. They had enough time to let passers-by know who they were, and, on the escutcheons, where they had fought.*

In March, Grant outlined his strategic plan to Meade; "Lee's army is your objective. Wherever Lee goes, there you will go also." While the Army of the Potomac was concentrated in central Virginia, ready to begin its campaign when the roads improved, Grant sent Union forces into the Shenandoah Valley, hoping to seal it off as an invasion route, and to deny the Confederates access to their "breadbasket." What followed was a campaign unlike any other. While Lee's men fought and fought well, Grant realized that while he could afford to suffer casualties, Lee could not. Also, as long as Grant kept on moving south, Lee would have to follow him. These were the cornerstones of Grant's campaign of 1864.

On May 4th the Army of the Potomac crossed the Rapidan River and entered the Wilderness, the scene of the Battle of Chancellorsville the year before. Lee realized that by fighting the Union army while it was still in the Wilderness, he could partly offset his opponent's superiority in numbers. He marched east to intercept Grant, the battle beginning early on May 5th when Ewell's Corps made contact with the right wing of the Union army near Wilderness Tavern, the site of Grant's headquarters. A.P. Hill's Corps deployed on Ewell's right, on the Orange Plank Road, where its advance was blocked by Hancock's II Corps. Hill was in poor health, but retained control of his command for the duration of the coming battle. Despite considerable success, the Confederates soon discovered that the defenders were more numerous and better prepared than they expected, and progress ground to a halt. Sedgwick's VI Corps bore the brunt of Ewell's attack, supported by Warren's V Corps and Burnside's IX Corps. Grant planned to pin down the attackers, while the rest of the Army of the Potomac was kept

Following pages: *Meade had sent Hancock down from Ely's Ford towards Chancellorsville, while Warren's V Corps and Sedgwick's VI Corps moved on the Germanna Plank Road. It became clear that Lee would meet them before they could march through the Wilderness, so Meade turned west to meet Ewell's approaching Confederates along the Turnpike, while Hancock moved towards Lee's flank and Sedgwick came up on Warren's right. For most of May 5th, two main battles raged: Ewell against Warren and Sedgwick on either side of the Turnpike, and Hancock against Hill on the Plank Road. Neither proved decisive. The next day, Grant planned a major assault, but Lee moved first against Sedgwick's right flank and then Hancock's left, almost breaking through. But the Confederates were a spent force, and Grant had decided that this battle had run its course. A decisive result was now beyond reach.*

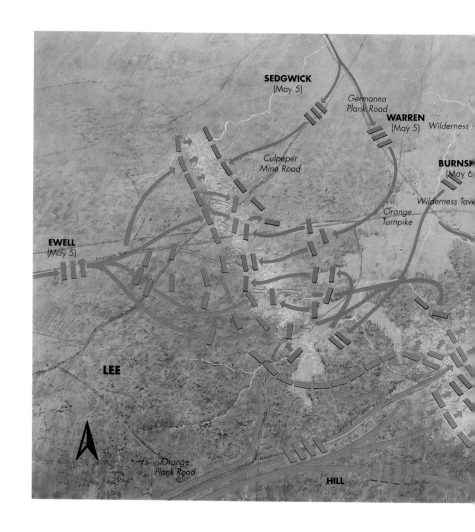

SEDGWICK
(May 5)

Germanna
Plank Road

WARREN
(May 5) Wilderness

Culpeper
Mine Road

BURNSI
(May 6

Wilderness Tave

Orange
Turnpike

EWELL
(May 5)

LEE

Orange
Plank Road

HILL

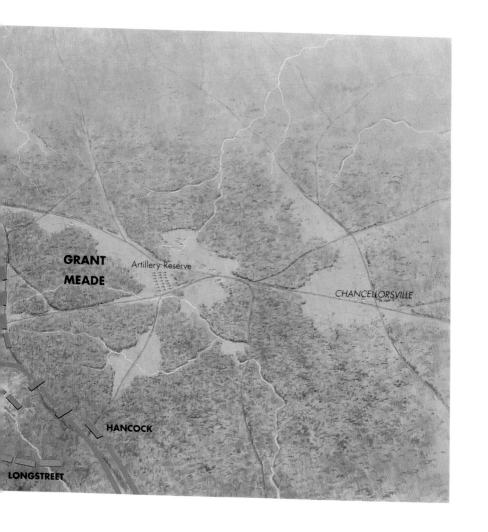

GRANT
MEADE

Artillery Reserve

CHANCELLORSVILLE

HANCOCK

LONGSTREET

Above: *A Union field artillery battery at the Battle of Cold Harbor, June 1864.*

back to counterattack when the moment was considered ripe. Meanwhile Getty's VI Corps seized the important intersection of the Orange Plank Road and the Brock Road, pinning the southern flank of the Union line. Given the virtually impassable terrain of the Wilderness, control of the few roads intersecting the area was vital in the battle that followed, and Grant realized this. By nightfall the Confederate attacks had waned, and the Army of the Potomac was able to consolidate its front line running north–south to the west of the Brock Road and Germanna Ford Road. Longstreet had still not arrived in the Wilderness, and dawn found the Confederates under pressure on both roads, as Warren advanced along the Orange Turnpike, and Hancock along the Orange Plank Road.

Ewell managed to hold his ground, but A.P. Hill's defense was broken, and his men fled to the rear. Lee rode into the clearing of the Tapp farm beside the Orange plank Road and tried to stop the rout. Just when he feared the worst, the Texas Brigade of Longstreet's Corps marched into view.

Reinforcements had arrived in the nick of time, and with Longstreet's arrival the Confederate right wing was saved. Lee remained in the frontline until the men beside him began shouting; "Go back, General Lee! Lee to the rear!" A Texan sergeant took the reigns of Lee's horse Traveller, and escorted his commander to safety. Once behind the line Lee met Longstreet, and after a short conference the corps commander gave orders for an immediate counterattack, spearheaded by the Texas Brigade. The unit broke through the Union line, but then found itself unsupported and surrounded. It was 20 minutes before the rest of Longstreet's Corps arrived to rescue it, by which time two-thirds of the Texans had been killed or wounded. Throughout the rest of the morning Longstreet continued his push forward, his troops fighting through the undergrowth on both sides of the Orange Plank Road and driving the Union lines back. Grant realized that Hancock's Corps was in trouble, and ordered Burnside's IX Corps to march to its support, but it took the lethargic Burnside most of the day to cover the three miles to the front. This allowed

Lee to maintain his pressure all along the Union line, as Ewell managed to advance steadily along the Orange Turnpike while Longstreet did the same to the south. By late-morning Longstreet discovered that Hancock's left flank ended just south of the Orange Plank Road, and was unsupported. Longstreet concentrated his attack there, and soon the southern flank of the Union troops was turned, forcing the defenders back to their final line of defense along the Brock Road. However, the success was short-lived, as Longstreet was accidentally shot by a Confederate soldier, and the attack faltered. Unlike Jackson, Longstreet would survive his wound; his corps would be temporarily assigned to Major-General Richard H. Anderson. Around noon the Confederates achieved the same success on Hancock's right flank, after a column of Confederate troops cut through the thickets to reach the northern end of the Union line. It was now 2pm. Then, to the north came Burnside's men. Although

they were almost eight hours late, they arrived when they were most needed, and were thrown into the attack against Longstreet's left flank. After heavy fighting just west of the Brock Road and Orange Plank Road intersection, Longstreet's left was driven back, easing the pressure on Hancock's shattered corps.

Lee was not done yet, and at 5pm he launched another assault on Hancock's position at the crossroads. Attacking over an abatis of felled trees, the Confederates were met by heavy musket fire all along the line, and the attack failed. To the north, Gordon's Division of Ewell's Corps managed to turn the right flank of Sedgwick's Corps, and it looked as if the Union defense of the Orange Turnpike would collapse. However, Union reinforcements arrived to save the day, and as night fell, the Confederate attacks ended. Although the battle was technically a Confederate victory that cost the Union side 18,000 men killed, wounded and missing, compared to the Confederates 11,000, it was still unclear what Grant would do next, and the outcome still hung in the balance. Unlike the commanders before him, Grant didn't retreat back over the Rappahannock River to lick his wounds. Instead, he gave the order to march south, closer to Richmond. The Union soldiers were demoralized after the battle, but when they found out they were heading south, the whole mood of the army changed. This was different. Grant would not let a defeat stand in the way of his strategic goal.

There was no fighting on May 7th, and as darkness fell Warren's V Corps left its position beside the Brock road and marched south, heading out of the Wilderness towards Spotsylvania Court House. The rest of the Army of the Potomac followed on behind. Lee had considered the

Below: *A Confederate trench dug at Cold Harbor. From 1864 onwards, the fighting became increasingly positional, and the smaller Confederate army was often forced to dig defensive trenches such as the one shown here.*

possibility that Grant might try to slip round him and had sent Stuart forward to patrol the roads leading south and east out of the Wilderness. His cavalry clashed with the Union troopers of Major-General Phil Sheridan at Todd's Tavern on the Brock Road, where the forest of the Wilderness gave way to open farmland. This confirmed Lee's suspicions, and he immediately ordered Richard Anderson, commanding Longstreet's 1st Corps, to march south via Shady Grove Church, in an attempt to reach Spotsylvania before Grant. He was followed by Ewell's Corps and A.P. Hill's Corps, now commanded by Major-General Early as Hill was incapacitated by illness. Both armies were now racing for the crossroads, but Stuart's calvary managed to delay the Union advance until Anderson arrived at Spotsylvania shortly after dawn on May 8th, blocking Grant's path.

For the next two weeks the armies fought for control of the crossroads, and the resultant combat was some of the fiercest and most bloody of the entire war. The Confederate entrenchments formed a large semicircle, with its center extending across the Brock Road, the apex of the line there being nicknamed "The Mule Shoe." This became the focus for Grant's attacks over the days that followed. He launched repeated assaults on the position, but each time the defenders succeeded in driving the attackers back. Then, during a pause in the fighting, Lee received intelligence that led him to believe Grant was planning to abandon the attack and march round Lee's position towards the south. He ordered the Confederate guns to be pulled back from the Mule Shoe, ready for the coming march to head off Grant's next move. Instead, Grant ordered another massed attack, and this time the defenders had no artillery support. Spearheaded by Hancock's II Corps the assault reached the

Mule Shoe, and the attackers fought their way in. Two other Union corps moved up to support Hancock, but it was Lee who reacted first, sending Gordon's Division of Ewell's Corps into the counterattack, an assault which drove the Union troops from the position. This time Hancock's men didn't retreat, but lay on the reverse slope of the earthworks, the two sides pouring fire into each other's ranks. Both sides fed whole brigades into this human meatgrinder, while the artillery of both sides added their weight to the struggle. While this was taking place Lee ordered that a new set of works be dug across the base of the salient, and at dawn on May 13th his men fell back and occupied this more secure position. Hancock's men occupied the Mule Shoe, only to find the interior of the earthwork position resembled a scene

Above: *Federal regiments carried two colors: a national flag and a regimental flag. Inevitably they were the focal point of hostile fire in battle. This regimental flag was presented to the 138th Pennsylvania Volunteer Infantry by the citizens of Bridgeport and Morristown, Pennsylvania during Christmas 1864. The battle honors of the Wilderness campaign can be see at the top.*

from hell. Bodies were piled up on top of each other, often trapping wounded men beneath them. Body parts were scattered everywhere, and the scene was one of wholesale carnage. One Union officer found the bullet-riddled body of a friend, whose left shoe alone was pierced by 11 bullet-holes. To the veterans who had experienced Antietam, Fredericksburg or Gettysburg, Spotsylvania was remembered as the worst battle of them all. Grant's attacks against a strongly entrenched position had been extremely costly, as the Army had lost over 10,000 men, but Lee had also lost 8,000 veteran troops, which he could ill-afford. For the next two days the survivors recuperated and prepared for a renewal of the bloody slaughter. However, Grant had other

Right: *The chaplain's quarters at Drewry's Bluff (Fort Darling) in April 1865. The battle here in May 1864 blocked the Union Major-General Benjamin Butler's attempt to capture Richmond.*

plans. He ordered his army to move slightly to the east, redeploying along a north–south rather than an east–west axis, which meant he faced the right flank of the semicircular Confederate position. On May 18th he launched a fresh attack from this side, but this was soon halted on discovering the Confederate position was too strong to take. That night he resolved to continue south towards the North Anna River, which lay between him and Richmond. By keeping moving, Grant was able to maintain the initiative, and while his losses were heavy, he could (unlike Lee) replace his casualties. Each defensive victory was bleeding the Army of Northern Virginia of strength, and Grant was aware that in a war of attrition he would be the victor.

The Siege of Petersburg
June 1864–March 1865

The city of Petersburg protected the southerly road and railway approaches to the Confederate capital Richmond. Grant's initial assault failed, and the arrival of Lee's reinforcements signalled the start of a protracted siege through the winter of 1864/65. The pressure on Lee continued in other areas, and he responded by sending Early to threaten Washington. The war of attrition began to take its toll though, and Lee abandoned Petersburg in April. Today, the site is preserved as Petersburg National Battlefield, part of the NPS.

Right: *The 13-inch "Dictator" mortar at the siege of Petersburg—possibly the most photographed cannon of the war.*

After failing to defeat Lee at Spotsylvania, Grant continued his march to the south, bypassing the Confederate army to move closer to Richmond. Apart from the Army of the Potomac, he could draw on two more Union forces; that of Major-General Sigel in the Shenandoah Valley, a small diversionary force of 8,000 men, and the 25,000-strong Army of the James, commanded by Major-General Butler. On May 15th Sigel was defeated at the Battle of New Market, a Confederate victory that was achieved in part with the help of the cadets of the Virginia Military Institute, who abandoned lessons to drive the Union troops from their valley. Ten days prior to this, Butler had landed his army at Bermuda Hundred and City Point at the confluence of the James and Appomattox rivers, south of Richmond and close to the neighboring city of Petersburg. After securing his bridgehead he advanced cautiously, allowing General Beauregard to move 20,000 Confederates into position to cover Richmond. By May 14th Butler had reached Fort Darling on Drewry's Bluff, a strong, entrenched position blocking the river and railroad approaches to Richmond from the south. While Butler pondered what to do next, Beauregard attacked him, driving the Army of the James back to its bridgehead. Butler was bottled up again in the narrow peninsula between the Appomattox and James rivers; his army was trapped, unable to advance. Grant would have to rely on Meade's Army of the Potomac to tip the strategic balance in his favor.

On May 23rd Grant's leading columns reached the North Anna River, only to find the Confederates had got there first. Although Lee had only 50,000 men, he used the river to his advantage, deploying in such a way as to force Grant to launch cross-river attacks that were unable to support each

other, allowing Lee to defeat each assault in turn. By May 26th Grant's army was on the move again, slipping away to the southeast across the Pamunkey River. After a major cavalry clash at Haw's Shop on May 29th, Lee discovered where Grant's army was located, and dug in between Grant and Richmond near the site of his first victory at Gaine's Mill two years previously. Lee's numbers were bolstered slightly by the Richmond garrison, and when Grant launched a massed attack on June 3rd, Lee was ready for him. In the Battle of Cold Harbor that followed, Grant hurled 60,000 men at the Confederate lines. In a day of heavy, incessant rain the defenders hurled back the Union assault. At the

Above: *Chaplains of the 9th Army Corps in the siege lines in front of Petersburg.*

height of the attack the Union army lost 8,000 men in eight minutes. It was the bloodiest charge of the war, and was no more successful than that headed by Pickett at Gettysburg the previous summer. A diary pulled from a dead soldier's pocket contained the poignant last entry: "June 3. Cold Harbor. I was killed."

Unable to defeat Lee in a frontal attack, Grant resumed his march southwards towards the James River. He planned to outflank Lee, but decided to avoid confining himself to the peninsula where McClellan's army was defeated in 1862. Instead he planned to cross the James River to attack Petersburg. He sent Major-General Smith's XVIII Corps by steamer to Bermuda Hundred, where Union engineers built a pontoon bridge across the Appomattox River. On the

Right: *Zuoaves of Company G, 114th Pennsyvlania Infantry at the siege of Petersburg, August 1864.*

afternoon of May 15th Smith's troops launched an assault against the northeastern corner of Petersburg's defenses, which succeeded in clearing the defenders from a portion of their earthworks. Grant's army crossed the river to City Point, and by June 16th some 75,000 men stood poised to launch a concerted attack against Petersburg's defenses, manned by General Beauregard and just 15,000 men. He drew men from the force blockading Butler's army, but reinforcements arrived from Richmond before the lethargic Butler could take advantage of the opportunity. On June 17th Grant launched his attack, but Beauregard's line just managed to hold on until on June 18th the leading elements of Lee's army arrived to reinforce him. Next, Grant ordered two corps to work their way round to the south of the Confederate

Above: A Federal musket cartridge box with shoulder belt.

position to cut the railroad leading south from the city, but A.P. Hill managed to defeat each force in turn. Faced with the inevitability of fighting a protracted siege, the Army of the Potomac began digging in, initiating a campaign that resembled the trench warfare of the First World War more than it did the more open fighting associated with the American Civil War. The siege that followed would last for just over nine months, and given the disparity in strength between the two armies, the outcome was hardly in doubt. Due to his lack of numbers Lee had sacrificed his mobility, and was forced to fight positional warfare, which allowed Grant to use attrition to swing the balance of the operation in his favor. At this stage of the war every Confederate loss was irreplaceable, while Grant seemed to have an unending supply of men, arms and supplies.

The only unpinned Confederate force in the Eastern Theater was the small corps of 9,000 men commanded by Major-General Early. Lee planned to use Early to divert Union efforts from Petersburg, and after sending the few reinforcements that could be spared, Lee ordered Early to launch a raid across the Potomac River. Early moved his 15,000 men north up the Shenandoah Valley, driving Sigel's beaten command out of Harper's Ferry and capturing the vast stockpile of supplies stored in the Union depot in the town. He then crossed the Potomac near Sharpsburg, sending his cavalry north to raid Hagerstown while he advanced on Frederick. Both towns were spared in return for the payment of an indemnity to cover Union depredations in the Shenandoah. By this stage Grant was alarmed enough to send Wright's VI Corps back from Petersburg to Washington, as the only Union troops between Early and Washington were the 2,000 men scraped together by Major-General

Above: A .*Federal 36-caliber Colt Model 1861 Navy revolver.*

Wallace (the author of B*en Hur*). Wallace took up a position on the east bank of the Monocracy River, a tributary of the Potomac that ran southwards from Frederick. Just before Early arrived to confront him, Wallace was joined by a division from Wright's Corps that had force-marched from its debarkation point in the Washington Navy Yard to the Monocracy River. On July 9th, Early's veterans assaulted the Union position and dispersed Wallace's ad-hoc corps, and by the next afternoon the Confederates were outside Washington. The city's defenses had been occupied by the remainder of Wright's Corps, and although Early captured Fort Stevens on the northwestern corner of the Union perimeter, the defenders managed to repulse the Confederate assaults. Finding Washington impregnable,

Below: A *dead Confederate defender lies in one of the trenches at Petersburg,* 1865.

Above: A Union artillery officer's insignia, belonging to Lieutenant G.W. Taylor of the 4th Massachusetts Battery.

Early marched his troops back across the Potomac into Richmond. While "Early's Raid" served to boost Confederate morale, it did little to alter the grim strategic situation facing Lee.

During the autumn and winter of 1864/65 Grant extended his lines westward to encompass Petersburg south of the Appomattox River. This stretched the defenders along a ten-mile arc of entrenchments, and cut the direct railroad links between Petersburg and the rest of the Confederacy. The biggest Union assault during this period came at dawn on July 30, 1864. Engineers had dug a 200-yard tunnel under the Confederate lines, and its head lay directly underneath a Confederate redoubt. The mine was packed with explosives. The plan was, when the mine exploded, Major-General Burnside's IX Corps would advance into the gap formed in the Union lines, creating a bridgehead through which the rest of the Army of the Potomac could pass. At 4.44am Petersburg was rocked by a gigantic explosion. The redoubt was demolished, and over 500 Confederate soldiers died in the explosion. Burnside ordered his men to attack, the assault spearheaded by Brigadier-General Ferrero's "colored" division. The attackers soon found themselves trapped inside the huge crater created by the explosion, while the defenders were able to line its edge and shoot into the mass of soldiers below them. It resulted in slaughter, but Burnside kept sending more troops into the same spot. Union soldiers clawed their way up the sides of the crater to fight the Confederates with their bare hands, but by mid-afternoon the attack was over; it was an unmitigated disaster that cost the lives of over 5,000 men. Other small battles and skirmishes would follow,

but none threatened to breach the Confederate perimeter.

Grant's army continued to receive reinforcements throughout the winter, and by late-February the besiegers outnumbered Lee's defenders by 125,000 men to 50,000. The Army of Northern Virginia was critically short of supplies, and elsewhere Union armies were dismembering the Confederacy, and starving the army of food and munitions. In the north, Major-General Sheridan had rampaged through the Shenandoah Valley, and Early had too few troops to stop him. Lee decided to risk everything on an offensive, and marshalled 25,000 troops in an attempt to break the Union siege and threaten Grant's supply base at City Point. Shortly

Above: A Union artillery battery at the siege of Petersburg.

Right: *Federal regulation drums belonging to New York, Vermont, and Massachusetts infantry regiments, together with a bugle.*

before dawn on March 25, 1865 Major-General Gordon launched an assault on Fort Steadman. The Union position was captured, but he was unable to progress any further, and the attack was abandoned, having cost Lee 2,700 men, the majority of whom had been taken prisoner during the Confederate retreat. A week later it was Grant's turn. He sent Sheridan west past Lee's lines to attack the Confederate rear. A skirmish at Five Forks on April 1st led to the turning of the Confederate right flank. Grant then attacked all along the line of entrenchments, and on April 2nd Wright's VI Corps pierced the city's defenses at Poplar Springs, an assault that cost the life of A.P. Hill.

That night Lee abandoned both Petersburg and Richmond, and led his dwindling army west along the north bank of the Appomattox River. His aim was to link up with General Johnston's army in North Carolina, but when Lee crossed to the south bank of the river he found his way south was blocked by Sheridan. Abandoning his supply wagons Lee marched around Sheridan to the west, only to lose his rearguard at Saylor's Creek on April 6th. The Army of Northern Virginia was now reduced to just 13,000 exhausted men. When Lee reached Appomattox Court House on April 8th he found Sherman had arrived there first. There was no other option left open to him. He told his staff: "There is nothing left for me to do but to go and see General Grant, and I would rather die a thousand deaths."

The following day, on April 9th, 1865, General Robert E. Lee met General Ulysses S. Grant in the parlor of Wilmer McClean's home in Appomattox Courthouse, and surrendered his army. Like his few remaining men, Lee had been worn down during the long winter in the trenches around Petersburg, and by the ruination of his home state.

After so much suffering, the end of the war and the slaughter must have been as great a relief to the vanquished as it was to the victors.

THE WESTERN THEATER

Shiloh (Pittsburg Landing)
April 6–7, 1862

Shiloh was the first major battle in the Western Theater. The Federal victory owed much to its strength in numbers, and the Confederates were steadily pushed back to Corinth, resulting in the eventual loss of the city. The battle was the bloodiest encounter so far, with over 13,000 Federal and 10,000 Confederate casualties. Shiloh National Military Park was established in 1894 to preserve the scene of the battle. The park is located in Hardin County, on the west bank of the Tennessee River, about nine miles south of Savannah, Tennessee.

Right: *A line of cannons at Shiloh National Military Park.*

Following pages: *On the first day, the advance of Johnston and his four corps (upper left) soon became disorganized as they struck Sherman's camps. Grant tried frantically to rally his surprised army, but it was Prentiss's action in the peach orchard, later known as the Hornet's Nest, that stopped the Rebel advance cold and bought precious time for the Union. Johnston committed his reserve early into battle, and was mortally wounded here. Sherman meanwhile tried to hold the Federal right against renewed attacks. The Hornet's Nest eventually fell, and the Union left flank collapsed. Meanwhile, Lewis Wallace began to approach from the far right, and Buell's marching divisions sped down from the north. The Confederates had pushed the Federals back to the Tennessee, but Beauregard lost his determination and called off the advance just as victory was seemingly within his grasp.*

In the Western Theater the opening moves of the Civil War were dictated by the neutrality of the state of Kentucky, the home state of both presidents, Lincoln and Davis. In September 1861 the Confederates advanced up the Mississippi River to occupy Columbus, Kentucky. In retaliation, a Union force under Brigadier-General Ulysses S. Grant occupied Paducah, Kentucky on the confluence of the Ohio and Tennessee rivers. The Confederate commander in the West, General Albert Sidney Johnston deployed his troops on a 170-mile front, stretching east from Columbus to forts Henry and Donelson guarding the Tennessee and Cumberland rivers, just south of the Tennessee state line, then on to Bowling Green, Kentucky. These dispositions may have looked good on paper, but a lack of troops meant that the Confederates were placed on the strategic offensive, and were vulnerable to a sudden concentration of Union forces.

This is exactly what happened. In conjunction with a squadron of Union gunboats, Grant launched a whirlwind offensive that forced the Confederates to abandon Fort Henry, a move that isolated Fort Donelson. Grant demanded the unconditional surrender of the poorly defended Confederate outpost, and Johnston then made the mistake of reinforcing its garrison, which only served to increase the enormity of the disaster when Donelson fell after a short siege. The Tennessee and Cumberland rivers were now wide open to the Union gunboats, and Commodore Foote promptly destroyed the railroad bridge over the Tennessee, severing communications between the towns of Columbus and Bowling Green. Johnston had no option but to withdraw south of the Cumberland River, followed by a small Union army commanded by General Carlos Buell, which occupied Nashville, Tennessee without a fight in late-February 1862.

The Confederate garrison at Columbus was also withdrawn, and by March 1862 the Confederate Army of the Mississippi had withdrawn into the middle of Mississippi, and was encamped around the strategic railroad junction of Corinth. Johnston's army was now at least concentrated in one place. He commanded a force of some 40,000 men, divided into three corps under Major-General Polk, Major-General Bragg and Major-General Hardee. Additional reinforcements were ordered to join the army in Corinth, as Johnston was determined to launch a counter-offensive that would drive the Union forces from Tennessee.

Above: *This photograph of a landing on the Tennessee River was taken in April 1862, a few days after the Battle of Shiloh. General Grant's headquarters boat, the* Tigress, *is tied up second from the right. Command of the river was vital for bringing up fresh troops and supplies.*

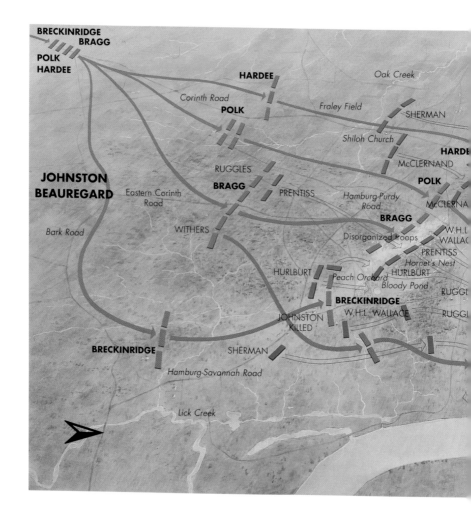

BRECKINRIDGE
BRAGG
POLK
HARDEE

HARDEE

Oak Creek

Corinth Road

Fraley Field

SHERMAN

POLK

Shiloh Church

HARDE

McCLERNAND

JOHNSTON
BEAUREGARD

RUGGLES

BRAGG

PRENTISS

Eastern Corinth
Road

Hamburg-Purdy
Road

POLK

McCLERNA

BRAGG

Bark Road

WITHERS

Disorganized troops

W.H.L
WALLAC

PRENTISS

Hornet's Nest

HURLBURT

HURLBURT

Peach Orchard

Bloody Pond

RUGGL

BRECKINRIDGE

W.H.L. WALLACE

RUGGL

JOHNSTON
KILLED

BRECKINRIDGE

SHERMAN

Hamburg-Savannah Road

Lick Creek

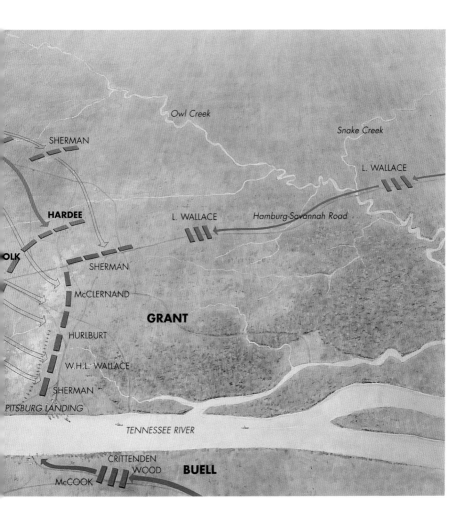

Owl Creek

Snake Creek

SHERMAN

L. WALLACE

HARDEE

L. WALLACE

Hamburg-Savannah Road

OLK

SHERMAN

McCLERNAND

GRANT

HURLBURT

W.H.L. WALLACE

SHERMAN

PITSBURG LANDING

TENNESSEE RIVER

CRITTENDEN
WOOD

BUELL

McCOOK

Above: *John Lincoln Clem. Clem was a 10-year-old drummer boy with the 22nd Michigan Infantry, whose drum was destroyed by a cannon ball at Shiloh. The Union press, anxious for heroes and inspiring stories from the battle, immortalized him as "Johnny Shiloh."*

By this time units of the Union army had reached Pittsburgh Landing on the Tennessee River, some 15 miles north of Corinth. Over the next few weeks Grant concentrated his army of 40,000 men there; his encampment was named Camp Shiloh after a church sited a few miles from the landing. Grant's superior General Halleck ordered Buell to march overland from Nashville to Pittsburgh Landing, thereby concentrating the Union army in one spot, where it would outnumber Johnston's Army of the Mississippi. When Johnston learnt of this, he decided to attack Grant before his army could be reinforced. It was now a race against time. The Confederate advance began on April 3rd and two days later the army was in position. Johnston had retained the element of surprise, as neither Grant nor his men had any idea the Confederates were so close. The Union commander even spent the night before the battle on a gunboat a few miles upriver, supervising the arrangements to receive Buell's reinforcements.

Johnston launched his troops into the attack at 6am on April 6th. The Union army was deployed in a series of divisional encampments: those of Sherman's 5th Division and Prentiss' 6th Division closest to Corinth near Shiloh Church; that of McClernand's 1st Division a mile behind them; and those of William Wallace's 2nd Division and Hurlbut's 4th Division close to Pittsburg Landing. Lewis Wallace's 3rd Division was deployed three miles north of the landing, close to the Mobile and Ohio Railroad. Buell's

18,000 men were still a day's march to the east, on the far side of the Tennessee River. This meant that as the Union troops were to be caught by surprised, the Confederates had a real chance of overwhelming Sherman's and Prentiss's divisions before the rest of the army could react to the sudden attack. The first Sherman's men knew of the assault was when a line of Confederates appeared out of the woods at the southern edge of their encampment. Within minutes two Union brigades had been completely overrun, and the rest of the two divisions were retreating north, pursued by Polk and Hardee's men. While many Union regiments fled to the safety of Owl Creek, to the northwest of Sherman's camp, some regiments managed to rally and gave ground stubbornly. The collapse was not total, however, largely thanks to the efforts of Sherman, and some semblance of a firing line was created on the crest of a small rise, which kept the attackers at bay long enough for McClernand's Division to join the fight. The Confederate advance was also hindered by the encampments themselves, as the attackers paused to plunder what they could before resuming the advance. Some men even stopped to eat the breakfasts abandoned by the enemy! Further east, Prentiss's men were also reluctant to give ground, and after retreating a little over a mile the remnants formed a defensive line, supported by the men of Hurlbut's Division. Finally William Wallace deployed his men to cover the gap in the center of the makeshift Union line. By 10am it was clear that the Confederate attack was slowing down, partly through the strengthening of Union resistance, but also because the densely wooded terrain disorganized the attackers, and made it difficult for commanders to control what was going on. By this stage the Union line stretched from the Tennessee River along a line

Above: *A pair of Federal drumsticks, together with a carrying harness that would be slung around the body.*

just north of the Purdy Road towards Shiloh Church. The Union left wing was formed along the line of a sunken lane, which offered the defenders some form of cover, and that stretched from a peach orchard on the right to the position north of Shiloh Church where Sherman and McClernand were making their stand. The peach orchard and the sunken lane would see some of the fiercest fighting of the day, as both sides fought for control of these features, which were collectively dubbed "The Hornet's Nest" by the soldiers who fought there.

The Confederates suffered heavy losses during their first probes against the makeshift Union redoubt. Bragg gathered together even more troops, and shortly after noon he launched a full-scale assault. It was repulsed, as was a second assault two hours later. Increasingly frustrated, the Confederates launched two more assaults on the position during the afternoon. General Johnston rode up to direct the third assault, which he sent through the peach orchard. The general was struck and mortally wounded during the assault, and died on the field. Beauregard assumed command of the army, and immediately ordered another attack on the Union position. By this stage the Confederates had brought up artillery to pound the position, and the fire from both sides was pronounced. This time the units defending the peach orchard broke and fled to the rear, and the Confederates were able to turn the flank of the Union position. On the left the Union line was first pushed back, and then it collapsed, allowing Bragg's men to work their way round the sunken road, precipitating a general withdrawal of the Union left. Over on the right the line established by Sherman and McClernand was slowly driven back by Polk, leaving the Union center exposed to attack. By 5pm this had turned into

ULYSSES S. GRANT (1822–85)

Grant was one of the outstanding commanders of the Civil War, a man of courage, conviction and strategic genius. He was born on April 27, 1822 in Point Pleasant, Ohio, the son of a tanner. In 1839 he won a place at West Point, and graduated in the middle of his class. He fought in the Mexican–American War under General Zachary Taylor, but a struggle with alcohol marred his career. By the time of the oubtreak of the Civil War in 1861, Grant was a civilian, working in his father's leather store in Galena, Illinois. In September 1861 he was appointed as a Brigadier-General of Volunteers, and he swiftly demonstrated that his unreliable days were behind him by whipping his unruly volunteer regiment into shape. Grant's capture of forts Henry and Donelson in February 1862 opened up the west for the Union, and his costly victory at Shiloh was critical. As Lincoln put it, "I can't spare this man. He fights." Grant's capture of Vicksburg on July 4, 1863 sealed his reputation, and earned him the support of the President. After his victory at Chattanooga during the winter, he was placed in command of the entire army, allowing him to direct strategy at the highest level. It was his strategic vision that brought the war to its conclusion, through the harrying and pinning of Lee in Virginia, the capture of Atlanta, and the subsequent "march to the sea" by Sherman. After the war Grant was seen as the country's premier soldier, and went on to become President of the United States (serving between 1869 and 1877). He remained a quiet, unassuming man, with, as Lincoln put it, a "habit of winning." Grant died on July 23, 1885 in Mount McGregor, New York.

Below: *Ruggles Battery at Shiloh National Military Park.*

a rout. William Wallace need not have worried about his right flank being exposed, as John Breckinridge was hurling forward every spare Confederate brigade in a frontal assault against the Union center. At first these attacks made little headway, but following the collapse of the Union left flank Wallace ordered his men to retreat back towards Pittsburg Landing. By 6pm the Union line had disintegrated, and the

exhausted Confederates sensed they were on the verge of winning a spectacular victory. However, they had neglected to consider Grant, who had arrived on the battlefield during the mid-afternoon, and who had spent the ensuing hours moving up reinforcements to form a final defensive line around Pittsburg Landing. This provided a rallying point for Sherman and McClernand who formed up on the right of the new Union line. Lewis Wallace's 6,000 fresh troops held the center, while the gunboats *Lexington* and *Tyler* helped protect the Union left by firing shells into any group of Confederates appearing close to the river. By this time all the combatants were exhausted and disorganized save those of Wallace, and his men formed an impenetrable barrier that kept the

Confederates at bay until nightfall. Shortly after 7pm Nelson's 4th Division of Buell's Army of the Ohio appeared opposite Pittsburg Landing, and his men were ferried across the river to form a reserve. A final Confederate assault was launched against the left of the Union line, but this was repulsed with the help of the gunboats. By dusk the attackers were too shattered to continue the fight. The Confederates had lost the opportunity to destroy Grant's

Above: A Light Artillery 12-pounder Model 1841 gun, surrounded by Federal artillerymen. This gun was the predecessor to the Model 1857 Napoleon gun.

army before Buell arrived, and with this they surrendered the initiative to Grant. The Army of the Mississippi had suffered over 12,000 casualties, a third of its strength, while some of the surviving units were too shattered to continue the fight. Beauregard's Army was in no position to resume the offensive.

The following day Grant launched a counterattack all along the line. Reinforced by Buell's three divisions, Grant had 25,000 men at his disposal, including Lewis Wallace's troops. He kept the rest of his shattered army in reserve. He had no need for them, as 25,000 fresh and well-equipped troops were more than a match for the exhausted and bloodied units of the Army of the Mississippi, whose effective strength was probably little more than 20,000 that morning. Although the outcome was inevitable, individual Confederate units displayed great courage, launching a series of desperate charges against the enemy to keep them at bay, and even managing to maul one of Buell's divisions which had advanced too far ahead of the rest of the army. Eventually Beauregard bowed to the inevitable and gave the order for the army to retreat. The Union pursuit was foiled by the disorganization of the two armies, and by the heavy rain which fell for two days following the battle. At the time, Shiloh was the bloodiest battle ever fought on American soil. Grant lost over 13,000 casualties, and allowed himself to be caught off guard, while Johnston paid the ultimate price for his gamble, as did a third of his army. After the battle, Halleck took control of the joint Union army, but he lacked Grant's zeal; it took him seven weeks to advance the 15 miles to Corinth. As for the Confederates, their strategy was in ruins, Tennessee was lost, and most of Mississippi lay open to the Union invaders.

Right: *This monument marks the site of Brigadier-General Stephen Hurlbut's divisional headquarters, at Shiloh National Military Park.*

Murfreesboro (Stones River)
Dec 31, 1862–Jan 2, 1863

Following the Battle of Perryville in October 1862, Bragg moved his Army of the Mississippi into Tennessee. Here he gathered his forces at Murfreesboro and formed the Army of Tennessee. William S. Rosecrans led the Union Army of the Cumberland in pursuit of Bragg, and the two armies clashed on the Stones River on December 30. Rosencrans claimed victory, but lost almost 13,000 men in the process. Today the site is preserved within the 600-acre Stones River National Battlefield.

Right: *Brig. Gen. J. C. Davis (left). His battle report observed "The troops suffered much from exposure. A heavy list of casualties and much suffering were unavoidable under the circumstances."*

Following pages: *Both
Bragg and Rosecrans planned
a major movement against
their opponent's right flank.
Bragg struck first. Early on the
morning of December 31 he
launched McCown's Division
against McCook's flank. The
whole Union flank gave way,
being pushed back nearly two
miles. A determined stand by
Sheridan's Division then
managed to anchor the failing
Union right. On the other side
of the field, elements of
Crittenden's Corps had crossed
Stones River, posing an
apparent threat to Bragg's own
right. Breckinridge's Division
remained there to cover the
flank for the whole morning. In
the center of the lines Bragg
had launched a series of
uncoordinated attacks against
an area called the Round
Forest, gaining good ground.
By the end of the day the
Union Army had been severely
mauled, but Bragg himself had
suffered heavy casualties.*

After the Battle of Shiloh the campaign in the West split into two parts. On the Mississippi River, Grant supervised a combined land and naval offensive down the river, while a similar naval campaign was conducted upstream from New Orleans. This strategically vital city fell to the Union on April 25, 1862, after Flag Officer Farragut led his fleet past the forts guarding the mouth of the river, and secured control of the lower Mississippi. The Confederates had already abandoned their defensive position at Columbus, and in early April General Pope captured Island No.10, a fort designed to stop any Union drive down river into Tennessee. A month later Fort Pillow fell, followed by the important river port of Memphis, Tennessee.

Over to the west, Buell occupied Corinth after the city was evacuated by Beauregard on May 29th. This secured western Tennessee for the Union, and let to Beauregard's replacement by Bragg. This coincided with Halleck's recall to Washington, and once more the Western Theater was deprived of an overall Union commander. Grant commanded the troops west of the Tennessee River, while Buell assumed command of those further east, all 31,000 of whom were incorporated into his Army of the Ohio. Buell's strategic aim was to secure all of Tennessee for the Union, which meant he had to isolate it from Bragg's army, secure the strategically important city of Chattanooga in southeastern Tennessee, and defeat the small Confederate force that occupied the far eastern portion of the state. After securing Corinth Buell advanced eastwards along the Memphis & Charleston Railroad into Alabama, reaching Decatur by mid-July.

In order to divert Buell, General Kirby Smith, the Confederate commander in eastern Tennessee, proposed marching north to invade Kentucky, rather than passively

wait to be cut off by the enemy advance. Bragg agreed with this somewhat ambitious plan, and leaving Major-General Van Dorn to watch Grant, he entrained his 30,000-strong Army of Tennessee (formed from part of the Army of Mississippi), and sent them south to Mobile, then north to Chattanooga. From there he could coordinate the coming offensive with Kirby Smith.

There the two Confederate forces were united under Bragg's command, giving him a force of 40,000 men. During August Bragg marched his men north, forcing Buell to break

Above: *After a fight exacting terrible losses on his command, Major-General Philip H. Sheridan finally brought a halt to the seemingly irresistible Confederate juggernaut at Stones River, providing an anchor for Rosecrans' ravaged forces on the Union right.*

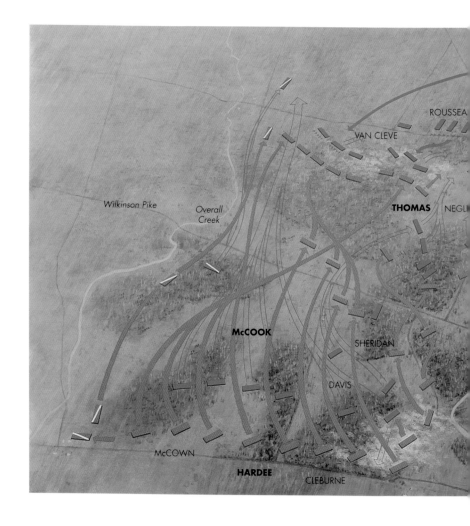

ROUSSEA

VAN CLEVE

Wilkinson Pike

Overall
Creek

THOMAS   NEGL

McCOOK

SHERIDAN

DAVIS

McCOWN

HARDEE   CLEBURNE

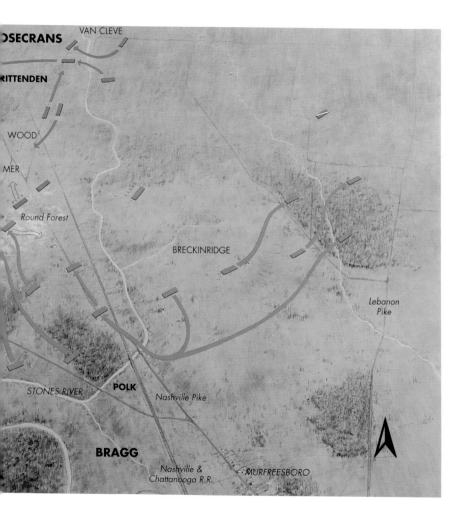

ROSECRANS

VAN CLEVE

CRITTENDEN

WOOD

MER

Round Forest

BRECKINRIDGE

Lebanon
Pike

STONES RIVER

POLK

Nashville Pike

BRAGG

Nashville &
Chattanooga R.R.

MURFREESBORO

Above: *Fighting from high ground with the assistance of massed artillery, Major-General Thomas L. Crittenden helped his leader Rosecrans record a narrow but morale-boosting victory over the Confederates at Stones River. Crittenden was one of the Union soldiers who had a brother (George) serving with the Confederates.*

off his drive into Alabama and move north. By mid-September Buell was in Bowling Green, but Bragg kept marching north, cutting Buell's rail links with the north. This prompted Buell to retire northwards to Louisville, where he was assured of reinforcements and supplies.

Meanwhile Kirby Smith's column had also entered Kentucky, marching north from Knoxville to reach Lexington. The Union commander expected Bragg to attack Louisville, but instead Bragg moved east to Perryville, where he linked up with Kirby Smith. Beuell was reluctant to attack Bragg, despite having 55,000 men under his command, but after Lincoln threatened to replace him, Buell marched out to meet Bragg. The two sides clashed at Perryville on October 8th. Bragg was away from the army when Buell approached, so Polk commanded the Army of Tennessee in his stead, and led an attack that repulsed Buell, but which caused substantial losses to both forces. For his failure, Buell was replaced by Major-General Rosecrans, while Bragg inexplicably retired back to his supply base at Chattanooga, abandoning all he had achieved that autumn.

Realising that Bragg had his limitations, President Davis appointed General Joseph E. Johnston as overall commander in the Western Theater, but refused to replace the commander of his main western army. Johnston also commanded General Pemberton's Army of the Mississippi, based in Vicksburg, Mississippi.

In December President Davis visited Bragg's army, and considering it was not under any immediate threat, he ordered the detachment of 10,000 men to join Pemberton.

This left Bragg with 35,000 men to face Rosencrans' 47,000 men, who were now at Nashville. Although it was winter, Rosecrans was under heavy pressure from president Lincoln, who wanted the Army of the Cumberland (the new name for the Union command in Tennessee) to resume the offensive. Rosecrans had already re-occupied Kentucky and central Tennessee, but any further advance was impossible while Bragg's army remained intact.

Rosecrans was helped by the news that Bragg had advanced from Chattanooga to Murfreesboro, and unlike Buell he wasn't reluctant to fight. On December 26th he marched the Army of the Cumberland out of Nashville, advancing slowly, as he had to fend off the cavalry forces of Brigadier-General Wheeler, which were screening Bragg's army. Four days later Rosecrans arrived on the western side of Murfreesboro, on the western bank of the Stones River to find that Bragg's 37,000 men were deployed northwest of the city, ready for action. Here the countryside was relatively open, interspersed with small woods and bisected by the river, which was easily fordable. The Army of Tennessee consisted of two Corps, so Bragg deployed Polk on the south bank, and split Hardee's Corps, deploying the bulk of it on the Confederate left, but leaving Breckinridge's Division north of the river.

Rosecrans had three Corps, and with 47,000 men at his disposal he enjoyed a significant numerical advantage. He deployed all three of his Corps on the south side of the river, with Crittenden's Corps on the left, Thomas' in the centre and McCook's on the right.

Above: General John C, Breckinridge was ordered by Bragg to attack overwhelmingly superior massed Union forces, including Crittenden's artillery on the high ground. It was madness: of just 5,000 men who commenced the advance, fewer than 3,500 came back.

Right: *General Braxton Bragg saw enemies everywhere. In the aftermath of the battle, he had them. His generals, including Breckinridge, Hardee, and Polk, went to war with him over his conduct of the fight; this was a "war" fought in headquarters tents, newspapers and the corridors of the South's War Department, and it surely played a part in the Confederacy's military downfall.*

Both commanders planned to attack the enemy on December 31st, with both opting to attack the enemy's left flank. However, it was Bragg who moved first, sending Hardee's Corps forward at dawn. The Union attack on Breckinridge was duly cancelled as a crisis overtook the army. Two of McCook's divisions were broken by the Confederate assault, but Sheridan's Division held firm, then withdrew in good order to form a secondary position along the Wilkinson Turnpike. This served to anchor Rosecrans' line, which was now bent back at right angles. Bragg then ordered Polk's Corps to attack Thomas' Corps to its front, and by 10am the Union Army was forced backwards into a cramped defensive line, its back to the river. Even Sheridan's Divison eventually fell back when it ran out of ammunition, and it seemed as if nothing could prevent the complete collapse of the army.

At that point Bragg ordered Breckinridge to attack Crittenden's Corps, the last unengaged portion of the Union army, deployed directly west of the Confederate right on the far bank of the river. During the morning Rosecrans had been moving units from his unengaged left wing to support his collapsing right, and this left Crittenden in a vulnerable position. Rather than launch a frontal attack, Breckinridge moved his troops to the right, and concentrated his force against the apex of the Union line, where Crittenden's eastward-facing line ended and Thomas' already demoralised men were formed up facing south. This was the hinge that could swing open the Union defence, the spot marked by a clump of trees known as "The Round Forest," but referred to by the participants as "Hell's Half Acre." Somehow the Union line held, the brunt of the attack falling on the brigade of Brigadier-General Hazen, whose men

defied all attempt to drive them from their position. This allowed Rosecrans to deploy his artillery reserve, the guns line up hub-to-hub. He was also able to bring up whatever reserves he could find to help Hazen, and throughout the afternoon Breckinridge launched an increasingly costly series of attacks, to no avail. As darkness fell on New Year's Eve it was clear that the Confederates had won a significant victory, but had failed to destroy Rosecrans' army. Both sides dug in where they were, the Confederates along the Wilkinson Turnpike, and the Army of the Cumberland a little to the north, astride the line of the Nashville & Chattanooga Railroad, with their flank protected by Stones River.

The two armies avoided fighting each other on New Year's Day. For his part, Bragg was convinced he had defeated Rosecrans sufficiently to make the Union commander retire from the field. It cam as a shock that the Union Army held its ground. The following morning (January 2, 1863) Rosecrans sent a division of Crittenden's Corps across the river to occupy a small hill that overlooked the right flank of the Union line. Shortly after noon Bragg responded by sending Breckinridge's men back across the river to attack this force, ignoring the reservations of his divisional commander.

At 4pm the assault crashed against the Union position, the defenders supported by massed artillery fire from across the river. Despite horrendous casualties, Breckenridge drove the defenders from the small hill, but this only exposed them to the full fire of the Union artillery, 58 guns firing at short range into the Confederate ranks. After a half hour of this, Rosecrans sent Negley's Divison from Crittenden's Corps across the river in an assault that broke Breckinridge's battered line, and drove the Confederates right back towards Murfreesboro. The Confederate attack ended in dismal failure, and Rosecrans' men had redeemed themselves following their ignominious defeat two days before.

Clearly Bragg could gain nothing from continuing the fight. His army had lost 12,000 men over the two days of battle, a third of his total force. Rosecrans' casualties were slightly higher, but he had the men to spare. The next day the Army of Tennessee retreated back to Chattanooga, leaving the battlefield, and most of Tennessee, in the hands of the enemy.

As for Rosecrans, he and his men considered themselves fortunate to have survived. They had managed to turn an initial Confederate victory into a bloody draw, but it was clear that while Murfreesboro had produced no clear winner, the Union emerged from the struggle in the stronger strategic position.

Although Rosecrans would need men and supplies to rebuild his army, a task that took him over six months, his presence at Murfreesboro allowed the Union to consolidate its hold on Tennessee. Eventually he would be able to resume his offensive against Bragg, whose army was confined to Chattanooga and Knoxville, the last Confederate-held parts of the state.

Far left: *Hazen Brigade monument, Stones River, is the oldest intact Civil War monument.* "THE BLOOD OF ONE THIRD ITS SOLDIERS TWICE SPILLED IN TENNESSEE CRIMSONS THE BATTLE FLAG OF THE BRIGADE AND INSPIRES TO GREATER DEEDS: ERECTED 1863 UPON THE GROUND WHERE THEY FELL."

The Siege of Vicksburg
May–July 1863

Vicksburg, the "Gibraltar of the Confederacy," occupied a key position on the Mississippi River. In early 1863 Ulysses S. Grant aimed to split the Confederacy in half by taking Vicksburg and Port Hudson, but he encountered formidable defenses. Several determined assaults failed, and a 47-day siege ensued. The Confederate defenders were slowly weakened by sickness and death, until Pemberton finally surrendered on July 3. Today the battlefield is preserved within the Vicksburg National Military Park.

Right: *The Missouri Monument, Louisiana Redan, Vicksburg. This memorial commemorates the 4,600 soldiers from the state who took part in the siege.*

Following pages: *The*
sweep of Grant's Vicksburg
campaign is readily evident in
the area needed to show his
movements. On March 31,
1863, McClernand's Corps,
followed by McPherson, began
heading south until they
arrived at Bruinsburg. Porter's
gunboats and transportshad
come down the river past
Vicksburg's batteries and
ferried the Union troops across.
A week later Sherman's Corps
made the same journey and
Grant was ready. He began
the overland campaign with a
brief sidestep to Grand Gulf,
then drove for Raymond. From
here he went north and took
the state capital, Jackson.
Having driven Pemberton's
forces back, Grant invested the
city on May 18th. Following
two unsuccessful assaults on
May 19th and 22nd, Grant
settled down to a patient siege.
Pemberton finally surrendered
the city on July 3rd, once he
had exhausted his food and
ammunition supplies.

In October 1862, General Grant became the commander of the Union Army of the Tennessee, charged with driving south down the Mississippi River from Memphis, Tennesee, to link up with the naval force commanded by Flag Officer Farragut advancing from the south. The only part of the river firmly still in Confederate control was Mississippi, from Vicksburg in the north to Natchez in the south. Confederate garrisons and some naval vessels still lurked up several tributaries, such as the Arkansas, Yazoo and Red Rivers, but these were little more than irritations. The real core of the Confederate position was Vicksburg, Mississippi, the river port forming a last link between the Trans-Mississippi Department of the Confederacy to the west of the Mississippi River, and the rest of the Confederacy to the east. By capturing Vicksburg, Grant would fulfill Lincoln's strategic goal of cutting the Confederacy in two.

His army of nearly 40,000 men was based at Grand Junction, Mississippi, some 30 miles east of Memphis, and a similar distance west of Corinth. Here Grant pondered his next move. Clearly he needed to invade western Mississippi, but while the strategic importance of the Mississippi River was uppermost in his mind, he still favoured a conventional land offensive, which would allow him to make use of the Mississippi Central Railroad as his main line of supply. Opposing him was Major-General (soon to be Lieutenant-General) Pemberton, with his 22,000-strong Confederate Army of the Mississippi. However, it was the Confederates who would begin the campaign, when a force of 27,000 men under the joint command of Major-Generals Van Dorn and Price advanced on the town of Corinth, a vital link in the line of supply and communications that linked the armies of Grant and Buell. The town was defended by Major-General

Rosecrans' Division, and on October 3rd the Confederates attacked. Rosecrans fought a skillful defensive battle, and although the Confederates forced him back, he managed to counterattack and defeat his assailants. In November Grant began his move south, driving Pemberton back before him. Grant captured Holly Springs, which he turned into a forward supply base, then continued south towards the important rail junction of Granada in central Mississippi. Despite Pemberton's withdrawal, Grant was not to have everything go his own way. The Confederates enjoyed a

Above: *A portion of the impressive river fleet commanded by Flag Officer David Dixon Porter in the bombardment of Vicksburg. One of the mighty City-class ironclads, originally named* St. Louis, *sits second from left.*

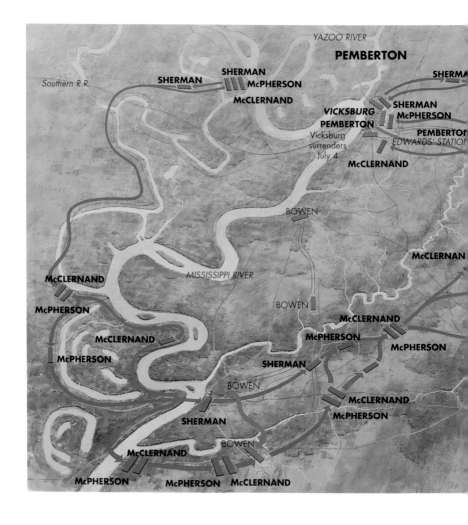

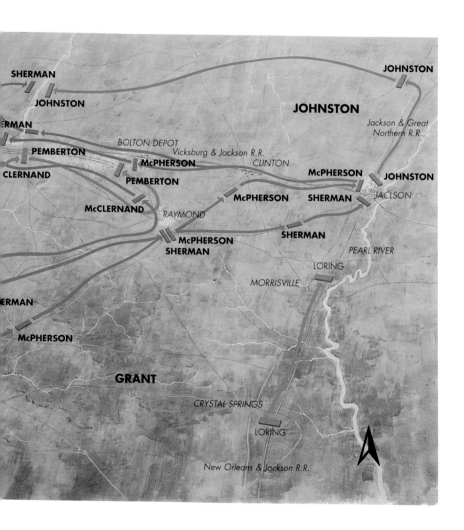

SHERMAN

JOHNSTON

JOHNSTON

JOHNSTON

RMAN

BOLTON DEPOT

Vicksburg & Jackson R.R.

Jackson & Great
Northern R.R.

PEMBERTON

McPHERSON

CLINTON

McPHERSON

JOHNSTON

CLERNAND

PEMBERTON

JACLSON

McCLERNAND

RAYMOND

McPHERSON

SHERMAN

McPHERSON

SHERMAN

SHERMAN

PEARL RIVER

LORING

ERMAN

MORRISVILLE

McPHERSON

GRANT

CRYSTAL SPRINGS

LORING

New Orleans & Jackson R.R.

qualitative advantage in cavalry, and Pemberton made the best possible use of this to disrupt Grant's plans. He sent Van Dorn around Grant's flank with a force of 3,500 cavalry, and on December 20th these troopers descended on the supply base at Holly Springs. After routing the garrison, Van Dorn's men destroyed the Union supplies, before retiring eastwards before Grant could react. Further to the north, the legendary cavalry commander Major-General Forrest led another force of 2,500 Confederate troopers into Tennessee, looping around Corinth to fall upon the Union railroad base at Jackson. In the process Forrest's men ripped up over 60 miles of track and cut down telegraph poles, cutting Grant's army off from the north. Grant had been outmaneuvered. He was forced to divert a significant portion of his army to re-establish and then safeguard his lines of communication, and, stripped of supplies, he retreated back north to Grand Junction. Grant's first drive on Vicksburg had ended in failure.

While Grant's offensive from the north was grinding to a halt, another Union attempt on Vicksburg also came to naught. Major-General McClernand was an influential politician from Illinois, and he persuaded Lincoln to allow him to raise a Corps-sized volunteer force in the Midwest, with the sole objective of capturing Vicksburg. By November these raw troops had gathered at Memphis. While Grant felt they were too inexperienced to assault Vicksburg, they could prove useful in diversionary attacks down the Mississippi, which would draw forces away from the main Confederate Army. He gave McClernand's Corps its baptism of fire by letting it attack Arkansas Post, a fort guarding the Arkansas River. With the help of naval gunboats McClernand's men captured the fort, and took 5,000 prisoners. While

Above: *Louisiana Stockade Redan, Vicksburg. The Union failures on May 19 and 22 to overrun this fortification were major factors in Grant's decision to avoid any more direct assaults.*

McClernand was occupied to the west of the Mississippi, Grant sent Major-General Sherman downstream to attack Vicksburg itself. Sherman began his journey down river on December 20th, the day Van Dorn attacked Holly Springs. Five days later he disembarked his force of some 15,000 men on the Yazoo River, a few miles north of Vicksburg, then launched them into an attack on the Confederate position at Chickasaw Bluffs. While Sherman was moving south, Pemberton moved his army south to cover Vicksburg, relying on his cavalry to pin Grant in northern Mississippi. He also received reinforcements, a division of 10,000 men that President Davis had ordered Bragg to release from the Army of Tennessee to bolster Pemberton's command. It was these men whom Sherman met when he crossed the Yazoo River to attack Vicksburg's defenses from the north. The Union assault was a failure, which cost Sherman 2,000 men for practically no cost to the Confederates. Clearly this approach to Vicksburg was no more viable than the overland route, and Grant would have to come up with a new scheme.

By this stage McClernand had joined Sherman, and assumed command, a move that alarmed both Sherman and Grant. After seeing to the defense of western Tennessee, Grant brought the rest of his army downriver to join McClernand, concentrating 60,000 men for an assault on the city. He was now committed to an attack on Vicksburg from the Mississippi rather than overland. This time it would come from the south, where Pemeberton least expected it. The conditions in the area were far from ideal. Most of this area of the Mississippi River consisted of muddy swamps, stagnant bayous and fever-infested backwaters, a breeding ground for disease and a demoralizing environment in which to campaign. However, conditions would be equally bad for the Confederates, while Grant at least had the advantage of the US naval control of the river, giving him the chance to strike where he wanted. First, Grant reorganized his army, creating three approximately equal-sized corps under Sherman, McClernand and Major-General McPherson. Next he sent expeditions to probe the Yazoo and its tributary waterways to the northeast of Vicksburg, looking for a way to outflank the Confederate entrenchments that lay along the bluffs north of the city. No suitable avenue of attack was found. Meanwhile Grant ordered an abandoned

canal to be re-cut in order to bypass Vicksburg. This allowed him to send supplies and men around the city. All this probing, engineering work and reconnaissance helped convince Grant that the only way to take the city was to bypass it, then land a force which would march north and capture it from its undefended southern side. To achieve

Above: *The unsuccessful Union attack upon the Confederate defenses of Vicksburg, May 19, 1863.*

Right: *Major-General John G. Parke, commander of the Union IX Corps Parke's Corps was part of the reinforcements sent to assist Grant during June. His men took part in the siege of Vicksburg, but saw no significant action.*

this he had to move Flag Officer Porter's fleet and the transports past Vicksburg. Too deep to use the new canal, they would have to force their way past Vicksburg itself. On the night of April 16th Porter made his move, his ironclad gunboats leading the way, or screening the vulnerable wooden gunboats and transports that made up the bulk of his fleet. It took an hour to run the gauntlet of Confederate fire, but apart from one transport and a few supply barges, the fleet made the passage relatively unscathed. Grant could now put his grand plan into operation.

He intended to march 42,000 men south to Hard Times landing on the west bank of the river, some 20 miles below Vicksburg, and just above the well-fortified river port of Grand Gulf. Porter's fleet would then transport the army across the river, where it could then march north to assault Vicksburg from the landward side. This was a risky operation, but the march to Hard Times was achieved without incident, covered by a diversionary attack launched by Sherman north of Vicksburg to pin the city's garrison in place. Porter's gunboats were unable to silence the Confederate batteries at Grand Gulf, so the transports had to run past the town and endure the enemy fire before they could reach Grant's intended landing place at Bruinsburg, some eight miles further downstream. Grant's men were disembarked on April 30th, and the following day they defeated a small Confederate force at Port Gibson, cutting Grand Gulf off from the hinterland of Mississippi. While Grant was landing his army south of Vicksburg, another diversion was undertaken by the Union cavalry commander Brigadier-General Grierson. He led 1,500 Union troopers south from Grand Junction into Mississippi, riding clear across the state and around the Confederate Army to reach

Following pages: *Fight in a crater made by the explosion of a mine under a portion of the Confederate works. As the siege progressed throughout June, Grant attempted to break through the Confederate defenses by mining under them and blowing them up.*

the safety of Louisiana, where they joined up with Major-General Bank's force, which was at Baton Rouge.

Grant's army spent two weeks marching up through Mississippi, cut off from its supply bases on the river. It was a gamble, but one that Grant saw as vital if he was to achieve the spectacular results he hoped for. By May 14th Grant reached the state capitol of Jackson, 30 miles east of Vicksburg. He then turned west along the line of the Vicksburg & Jackson Railroad, while detachments worked their way north, opening up a rail line to Grand Junction, some 180 miles away in Tennessee. Two days later Grant found his way blocked by Pemberton with 22,000 men, but lacking his high-quality cavalry, the Confederate commander remained unaware that Grant was nearby until Union columns appeared in front of him, and on his flanks. The battle cost Pemberton 4,000 men, and ended with his army in retreat. Grant lost 2,400, but was able to resume his pursuit, fighting off a rearguard action at the Big Black River the following day, and by the afternoon of May 18th his leading troops were standing outside Vicksburg's ring of defenses. Pemberton drew his remaining 30,000 men into the city's perimeter, and Grant invested the city with his 32,000 men, a force that would increase to 41,000 a week later.

At first Grant tried to smash his way into Vicksburg, launching a major assault on the northeast corner of the defenses on May 19th, which was repulsed with heavy losses. Undeterred, Grant ordered another attack three days later, this time hitting the centre of the Confederate line. Once again the Union attackers were repulsed, and McClernand's conduct that day would eventually lead to his dimissal as a corps commander. It was clear that the city's

defenses were too strong for Grant, but he had the city surrounded, while Porter's fleet cut Vicksburg off on the river. The Union commander would just have to wait. While his men dug siege works around the city, Grant landed his heavy guns, and soon the city was under near-constant bombardment by artillery and mortars, and also the occasional naval bombardment by the Union fleet in the river. The siege lasted for 48 days, with conditions in the trenches becoming increasingly desparate for the defenders, and, despite the efforts of General Joseph E. Johnston, the Confederates lacked the troops to send an army to lift the siege. The outcome was inevitable. By the start of July the city's population and the garrison had run out of food, and the troops were woefully short of ammunition. On July 3rd Pemberton raised a white flag and asked to discuss surrender terms. The following day, Grant rode up to Pemberton's headquarters and formally accepted the surrender of Vicksburg. All 30,000 soldiers of the Confederate Army of the Mississippi were taken prisoner, a blow to the Confederate cause from which it would not recover. With the capture of Vicksburg Grant had succeeded in the strategic war aim of conquering the Mississippi River, and in so doing, splitting the south in two. With the Mississippi secured, Grant and his colleagues in the Western Theater could concentrate on the destruction of Bragg's Army at Chattanooga, and on taking the war deeper into the Confederate heartland. Ironically, on the same day that Pemberton offered to surrender his army at Vicksburg, General Robert E. Lee was leading his army south from the blood-soaked ground of Gettysburg. That July, the Confederacy suffered two grievous defeats, and while the war would continue, the issue was now no longer in doubt.

Left: *The Illinois Monument, Vicksburg. Modeled after the Pantheon in Rome, this memorial is the largest in the Vicksburg National Military Park.*

Chickamauga
September 18–20, 1863

In September 1863, the Federal
William S. Rosecrans drove Braxton
Bragg's Confederates out of
Chattanooga. Bragg sought to
reoccupy the city by defeating
Rosecrans in battle. Bragg's first
assault faltered. The next day, he
continued his attack and, with the aid
of James Longstreet, broke through.
The Confederate victory forced the
Union troops to retire to Chattanooga,
trapping the Army of the Cumberland
there. Today the site is preserved
within the Chickamauga and
Chattanooga National Military Park.

Right: *The Federal Lieutenant Van Pelt defending his battery at
Chickamauga. Pelt would be killed soon after.*

After the Battle of Murfreesboro Rosecrans' Army of the Cumberland remained in the city he captured for another six months, while Bragg's Army of Tennessee lay encamped just 30 miles around Tullahoma, blocking any Union advance towards Chattanooga. The Confederate general had been roundly criticized for the missed opportunities of Perryville and Murfreesboro, and his soldiers had little faith in his abilities. While Lee was winning victories in the Eastern Theater, Bragg appeared willing to surrender the initiative to his enemies in the West. Rosecrans was also subject to criticism for failing to take to the offensive, seeming content to build up the strength of his army but not to use it.

It was late-June before Rosecrans took to the offensive, sending his army forward in four columns and initiating a series of bold flanking maneuvers that would force Bragg to withdraw down the line of the Nashville and Chattanooga Railroad towards the Tennessee River. Chattanooga was of crucial strategic importance, as it formed the focus of a rail and river transportation system that linked the Eastern and Western theaters, and which in Union hands would provide a springboard for the invasion of Georgia, Alabama and eastern Tennessee. Every time Bragg stopped to give battle, Rosecrans found a way to send one of his corps around the Confederate flank. By mid-August Bragg had crossed the Tennessee River into Chattanooga, while Rosecrans halted his army on the north bank of the river and brought up supplies. That same month, Rosecrans crossed the river west of Chattanooga, then advanced on the city, at which point Bragg abandoned it without a fight, moving 25 miles south to Lafayette, Georgia. This was a ruse to make Rosecrans believe the Army of Tennessee was in headlong

retreat, and the Union commander took the bait, sending his three corps (XIV under George Thomas, XX under Alexander McCook, and XXI under Thomas Crittenden) south in pursuit. This time Bragg planned to stand and fight. Not only had he just been reinforced by 9,000 men from eastern Tennessee under the command of Simon Buckner, but Lee also dispatched Longstreet's Corps (who two months previously had been fighting on Lee's right flank at Gettysburg) to the Western Theater. This would give Bragg a slight superiority in numbers over his opponent (66,000 men to 58,000), and he had the benefit of surprise on his side. Rosecrans' army was advancing into a trap.

Above: *Part of the Chickamauga battlefield. Just two days of fighting resulted in some 16,000 killed, wounded or missing Federal soldiers, and 21,000 Confederates.*

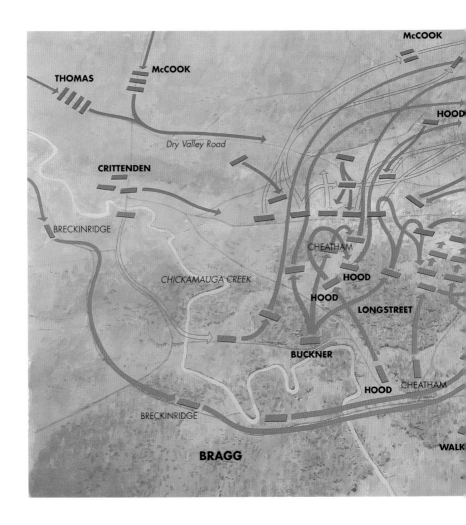

McCOOK

THOMAS

McCOOK

HOOD

Dry Valley Road

CRITTENDEN

BRECKINRIDGE

CHICKAMAUGA CREEK

CHEATHAM

HOOD

HOOD

LONGSTREET

BUCKNER

HOOD   CHEATHAM

BRECKINRIDGE

BRAGG

WALK

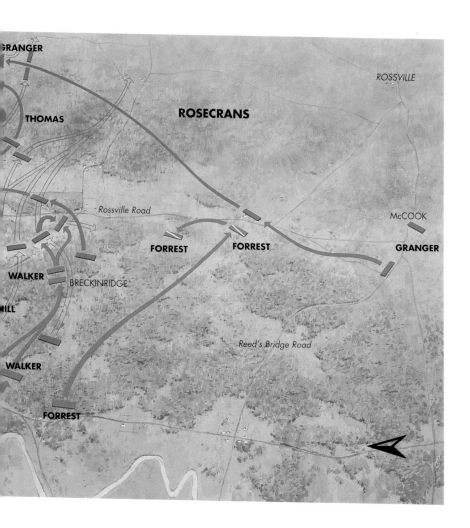

Previous pages: *The fighting at Chickamauga took place on an extended battleline almost five miles wide. The fighting rolled gradually from the south end toward the center throughout the first day. A substantial attack by Stewart nearly penetrated the Federal line, as did Hood's brutal assault on Rosecrans's right flank. The Union line held though. The day ended with Cleburne's twilight attack at the opposite end of the field. The next day Bragg intended a general attack starting on his right and moving to his left. In obedience to confused orders, Thomas Wood's command pulled out of the Union center, opening a massive gap just as Longstreet's men approached. The Union right collapsed and fled for Chattanooga. Thomas's defense of Snodgrass Hill was vital in buying time for the Federal retreat.*

Right: *A collection of typical Federal campaign matériel, in Virginia, 1864.*

Unfortunately, Bragg was not able to spring it. On September 11th he gave orders for his units to attack Thomas' isolated XIV Corps, but his men failed to respond in time. By the 13th Rosecrans had discovered how vulnerable his army was, and gave orders for it to concentrate on the position held by the 14,000 men of Crittenden's XXI Corps on Chickamauga Creek. Having failed to trap Thomas' XIV Corps, Bragg's army found itself to the east of Chickamauga Creek, which placed it on the flank of any force that would be marching north to join Crittenden. Inexplicably, instead of attacking the Union columns individually as they marched north to join Crittenden, Bragg decided to march north himself, passing beyond Crittenden's position at Lee & Gordon's Mills to place his army between Rosecrans and his supply base at Chattanooga. Certainly he was still waiting for the rest of Longstreet's men to arrive, but the opportunity presented by Rosecrans' scattered deployment was simply too good to miss. It was a wasted opportunity that robbed the Confederacy of a stunning victory—one that might have changed the course of the war.

By the morning of September 19th Rosecrans had managed to concentrate his army along the Lafayette Road, his men facing east towards Chickamauga Creek, the last known position of the Confederate Army. Crittenden's XXI Corps was on the Union left, McCook's XX Corps was in the center, while Thomas' XIV Corps was marching north to take up position on the Union left. At the same time, Bragg's army was crossing the creek in several columns. Polk was screening Crittenden across the creek in the south, while Simon Buckner's and William Walker's corps were crossing Alexander's Bridge, placing them opposite the left wing of McCook's XX Corps. Further north Major-General John

Hood's corps (from Longstreet's command) crossed Reed's Bridge while Forrest's Cavalry Corps moved forward over Dyer's Ford. The Confederate advance was a cautious one, Bragg wanting to determine the extent of the Union line before committing his army to the attack. His objective was the Lafayette Road—Rosecrans' link back to his supplies in Chattanooga.

The battle began around 10am, when the dismounted troopers of Forrest's Cavalry Corps ran into the head of Thomas' XIV Corps on the Lafayette Road. Both Forrest and Thomas sent reinforcements, and the skirmish turned into a full-scale battle. This served to pin Thomas in position, allowing Hood to maneuver his men into position, and then launch them against Thomas' line drawn up in a semicircle in front of the Lafayette Road. Walker's Corps then joined the fight, and the Union line was driven back for almost a mile through the woods, until it lay just west of the road, in the vicinity of Snodgrass Hill. However, the Confederates were unable to break Thomas' line, and his troops still denied the Confederates the open use of the road to reorganize their scattered troops. Hood almost achieved a breakthrough when his men charged Van Cleve's 3rd Division of Crittenden's XXI Corps, which had been transferred to the north to bolster the Union line. The Union center was forced back and Van Cleve's units were routed, but a counterattack by Philip Sheridan's 3rd Division of McCook's XX Corps and Wood's 1st Division of Crittenden's XXI Corps managed to prevent a Confederate breakthrough, allowing troops from Thomas' Corps to restore the Union line. That afternoon the battle lines surged one way then the other, and both armies fought each other to a standstill in the blood-soaked woods. It seemed as if the outcome of

Murfreesboro was to be repeated, where Bragg's army would bring the enemy to the edge of breaking, but fail to deliver the knockout punch. Finally, in the late-afternoon, D.H. Hill's men arrived after force-marching from the railroad depot at Ringgold, Georgia, and Cleburne's Division of Hill's Corps

Above: *Lee & Gordon's Mill, Chickamauga. Bragg believed that the Union troops here were the northernmost elements of Rosecrans's force.*

was thrown into the action on the Confederate right. Known as the "Stonewall of the West," much was expected of the young Irish-born general, whose troops were probably the only fresh force left on the field. He drove the Union line back, but he was eventually brought to a halt by the combined firepower of two Union divisions. The battle drew to a close as darkness fell, the dark woods filled with the cries of the wounded. In the Cherokee tongue, Chickamauga means "The River of Blood." It lived up to its name.

That night Longstreet joined Bragg, allowing the army commander to reorganize his army. Both Longstreet and Leonidas Polk were given a wing to command, Polk's force consisting of D.H. Hill's Corps, Walker's Corps and Cheatham's Division, while Longstreet commanded Buckner's and Hood's Corps, each comprising three small divisions. The army was given orders to resume the attack the following morning, Polk on the right and Longstreet on the left. For his part Rosecrans stayed on the defensive. As his corps were now confusingly intermingled, he placed Thomas in command of those on his left, and McCook in command of those on his right, while Crittenden controlled his few reserves.

The second day of battle began at 9.30am with a Confederate attack on the Union left, Breckinridge's Division assaulting Thomas' northern flank. The defenders weathered the charge, and after an hour they managed to drive the attackers off. Next, Cleburne's Division attacked the same position, but again, the attack was repulsed with heavy losses after some bitter hand-to-hand fighting along the Lafayette Road. Polk was launching his attacks in a piecemeal fashion, which did little to threaten the Union position. While this was taking place Forrest's cavalry tried

Below: *An assortment of Union medical officer uniforms and equipment, including surgical instruments.*

to work their way round the western flank of the Union line, but were stopped by the Union reserves.

The fighting in the north degenerated into long-range exchanges of fire, and the main focus of the battle shifted to the south, where Longstreet was scheduled to attack. At 11.30am Longstreet's wing advanced with 23,000 men, the

Below: *Knives used by the Confederate infantry.*

divisions of Johnston, Kershaw and Laws in the center, supported by Cheatham's Division on their right flank. Hindman's Division and Buckner's Corps formed a second wave behind and to the left of Hood's first line. The battle had already joined further north, and as he was not expecting an attack against his right, Rosecrans ordered Wood's Division to redeploy to the north, where it could support Thomas' Corps. McCook was just reorganizing his line to cover the resultant gap when Hood appeared at the head of his leading three divisions. Hood's men surged into the gap like a gray tidal wave, sweeping away any Union regiment that stood in their path. On Hood's left Hindman's Division smashed into Sheridan's Division, driving it from the field, while Buckner swept away Davis' Division. McCook's Corps had ceased to exist as a fighting force. The gifted Hood was wounded during the attack, but survived after having his leg amputated; he would rejoin the army in time to lead it on one last reckless adventure a year later.

Thomas rallied Brannan's Division, forming a cornerstone for his defense on the southern side of Snodgrass Hill, and so prevented his own command from being swept away in the rout. He managed to contract his line, forming a defensive perimeter along Horseshoe Ridge, which held off attacks from both Polk and Longstreet throughout the afternoon, earning Thomas the nickname "The Rock of Chickamauga."

Meanwhile, McCook's Corps swept half of Crittenden's reserve along with it as it was routed, and a mass of fleeing Union troops headed northwest through McFarland's Gap to reach the relative safety of Chattanooga. Longstreet was eager to pursue them, but Bragg held him back, stressing that Thomas' Corps was still on the field. At late-afternoon

Left: *A monument to the 18th U.S. Infantry Regiment at Chickamauga National Military Park.*

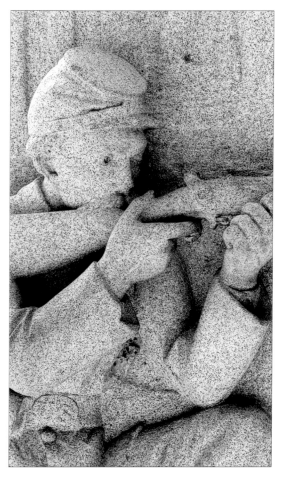

Left: *A detail from the monument to the 15th U.S. Infantry Regiment at Chickamauga National Military Park.*

Brannan's line on Snodgrass Hill still held, despite attacks from Hindman, Kershaw, Johnston and Preston's divisions. Critical to the defense of the hill was the return of part of the reserve, James B. Steedman's 1st Division, which had been deployed to the north to hold off Forrest's cavalry. Since Forrest had disengaged on Bragg's instruction in order to form a new reserve, Steedman was able to support Brannan, and the line held. A half mile to the east Thomas' battered line held until nightfall, despite being attacked from three sides. The return of Sheridan's Division down the Lafayette Road reopened Thomas' line of communications, allowing Rosecrans and Thomas to disengage, retiring to the north under cover of darkness. True to form, Bragg give no orders to pursue them.

Although Chickamauga was a spectacular Confederate victory, it was also a lost opportunity. As at Murfreesboro, Bragg had been given the chance to destroy Rosecrans' army, and he failed to do it, allowing the Army of the Cumberland to survive, ready to fight another day. If Longstreet had been allowed to pursue McCook, or if Forrest had been given orders to seal off Thomas' Corps from the north, the final outcome of the battle might have been very different. The cost of the victory was high. The Confederates lost 18,000 men killed or wounded, almost a third of the army. while Rosecrans lost 16,000 men; those troops that survived were badly demoralized, and unwilling to risk their lives in another costly battle. Chickamauga witnessed the bloodiest two days of continuous fighting of the whole war, but the butchery did little to alter the outcome of the Campaign in the West. The war would continue, and the Confederacy was running desperately short of men.

Chattanooga
November 23–25, 1863

❖

Realizing that Rosecrans's trapped forces had to be relieved, Hooker and Sherman were sent to Chattanooga in late-1863. Soon afterwards, offensive operations began against the Confederates. The key positions of Lookout Mountain and Missionary Ridge were taken from Bragg's troops, who withdrew to Georgia, while Chattanooga, the "Gateway to the Lower South," was secured as a vital supply and logistics base for the Union. Today the site forms part of the Chickamauga and Chattanooga National Military Park.

Right: *Federal troops on Lookout Mountain, overlooking the Chattanooga Valley and Tennessee River.*

Following pages: *Grant's breakout from Chattanooga proved to be one of the most spectacular affairs of the war. Bragg had neatly cut off all the supply routes to the city, and had placed his army in a semicircle stretching from Lookout Mountain to Tunnel Hill. To break out, Grant first struck Brown's Ferry in late-October. With this secured, a line of supply and reinforcement was open. In late-November, Grant moved forward to capture Orchard Knob, and then launched an assault on Lookout Mountain. In a spectacular engagement, he drove Breckinridge's thin lines from the crest, before conducting a grand assault on November 25th. Sherman moved across to strike Cleburne and others at Tunnel Hill, then Thomas swept forward up Missionary Ridge while Hooker struck Bragg's left flank. Breckinridge's Corps was soon put to rout, with only Hardee and Cleburne's rearguard action saving the army.*

Following his rout of the Army of the Cumberland at the Battle of Chickamauga, General Rosecrans retreated to his supply base at Chattanooga, less than ten miles to the north. For his part, General Bragg moved up to the city, and the Army of Tennessee established itself on the high ground of Lookout Mountain and Missionary Ridge, which overlooked the city, and where the Confederate guns could dominate the Union enclave below them. Chattanooga was now virtually under siege. The Confederate garrison sealed the city off from relief to the west, and gun batteries on the mountain swept the river, preventing any attempt to bring reinforcements or supplies to Chattanooga by steamer. The Confederate positions along Missionary Ridge covered any approach to the city from the east. Chattanooga lay in a bend in the Tennessee River, so effectively the Union army was trapped. Rosecrans' only option was to bring supplies into the city across the Tennessee River. Meanwhile he undertook no offensive operations to improve his position, and instead dug a substantial line of earthworks and redoubts across the neck of the river bend that enclosed Chattanooga. In effect he was stoppering the cork in his own bottle.

Although Rosecrans had proved himself to be a competent general, at least by Union standards, his defeat at Chickamauga seemed to have shattered his confidence, and removed any remaining trust his men had in him as a commander. Lincoln described him as being "stunned and confused, like a duck hit on the head." He was relieved of duty, and Major-General Thomas took over command of the army. After his redoubtable performance at Chickamauga, he was clearly the right man for the job. Lincoln also made two other strategic decisions that would have a profound

influence on the course of the campaign, and the war. Firstly, he ordered Major-General Hooker's Corps to detach itself from the Army of the Potomac at Manassas, and sent it west to join Thomas at Chattanooga. Secondly, and even more significantly, he promoted Ulysses S. Grant to command all the Union forces in the West.On October 23rd Grant arrived at Chattanooga to take command of the situation. Grant also changed the corps commanders of the Army of the Cumberland whom he regarded as having performed poorly at Chickamauga, and promoted the divisional commanders who fought well (major-generals Palmer and Granger.) Grant ordered Major-General Howard from the Army of the

Above: *The view from Lookout Mountain: what looks like an impregnable position.*

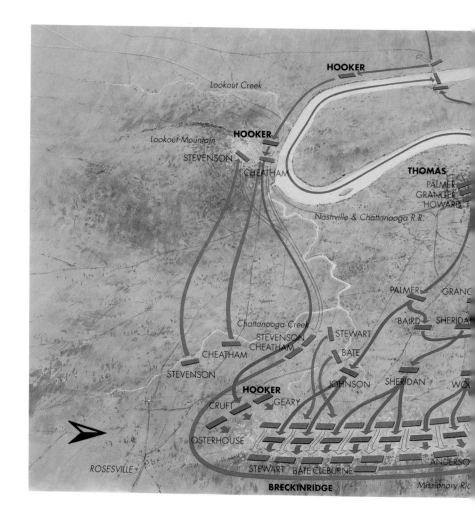

HOOKER

Lookout Creek

Lookout Mountain

HOOKER

STEVENSON

CHEATHAM

THOMAS
PALMER
GRANGER
HOWARD

Nashville & Chattanooga R.R.

PALMER   GRANG

BAIRD   SHERIDA

Chattanooga Creek

STEVENSON   STEWART
CHEATHAM
BATE

CHEATHAM

STEVENSON   JOHNSON   SHERIDAN   WO

HOOKER

CRUFT   GEARY

OSTERHOUSE

ANDERSO

ROSESVILLE   STEWART   BATE   CLEBURNE   Missionary Ric

BRECKINRIDGE

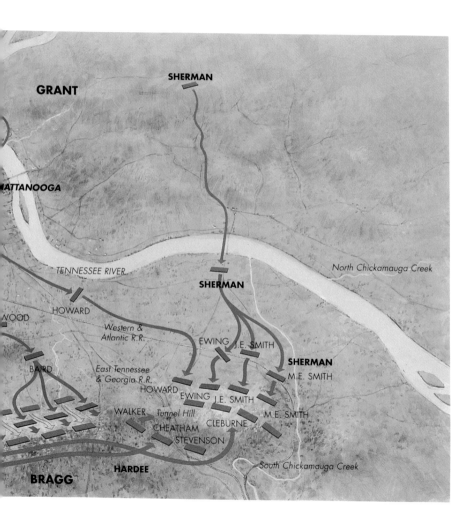

GRANT

SHERMAN

CHATTANOOGA

TENNESSEE RIVER

North Chickamauga Creek

SHERMAN

HOWARD

WOOD

Western &
Atlantic R.R.

EWING J.E. SMITH

SHERMAN

M.E. SMITH

BAIRD

East Tennessee
& Georgia R.R.

HOWARD

EWING J.E. SMITH

M.E. SMITH

WALKER Tunnel Hill

CLEBURNE

CHEATHAM

STEVENSON

South Chickamauga Creek

HARDEE

BRAGG

Potomac to take command of the third formation in Thomas' army.

Grant's first move was to secure a reliable line of supply into the city. Brigadier-General "Baldy" Smith proposed capturing the river crossing at Brown's Ferry, four miles downstream from the city, on the far bank of a loop in the river. This would allow Union supplies to be brought up without having to run the gauntlet of the guns on Lookout Mountain, two miles away to the south, at the southern end of the river bend. On October 27th Smith embarked a force of 3,500 men onto a small fleet of barges, then ferried them downstream in the darkness, passing under the guns on Lookout Mountain. Just before dawn the Union troops stormed ashore, driving off the Confederate skirmishers at Brown's Ferry to secure the position. The daring scheme paid off. Grant immediately ordered a pontoon bridge to be constructed across the Tennessee River, and by the end of the month Union supply wagons were rolling into the city once more. Hooker's force, XI and XII Corps from the Army of the Potomac, were deployed to guard the vital position at Brown's Ferry, and "Fighting Joe" not only protected the supply route, but also moved his 16,000 troops forward to Lookout Creek, pinning the Confederate flank at Lookout Mountain. The men of the Army of the Cumberland nicknamed Grant's new supply route "The Cracker Line." As supplies and reinforcements streamed into Chattanooga, Grant set about devising plans to raise the siege. Major-General Sherman was due to arrive in the city with 20,000 reinforcements from the Union Army of the Tennessee, giving Grant 70,000 troops for the coming operation. In contrast, Bragg's army was dwindling. He commanded a little under 70,000 men at Chickamauga, and when he first

invested Chattanooga he had 65,000 men in his army. Since then Longstreet's Corps of 15,000 men had been sent northeast to Knoxville, where it drove off a Union force that had occupied the city. From there he could move east to support Lee, or west to join Bragg's army if required, but the

Above: *The Chattanooga and Nashville Railroad Depot, at Nashville. The railroad provided vital communications and logistical support.*

real reason behind his redeployment was Longstreet's strongly-voiced criticism of Bragg, whom he regarded as incompetent. Indeed it was President Davis who suggested that Longstreet detach himself from the Army of Tennessee in an attempt to heal dissent in the army. Therefore when Grant made his move at Chattanooga, Longstreet was 200 miles away, kicking his heels in eastern Tennessee. This left Bragg with just 40,000 men. To balance the inferior numbers, his troops were dug in behind a line of substantial earthworks that ran along the crest of Missionary Ridge, and further protection was afforded by a forward defensive line that ran along the base of the ridge. Breckinridge's Corps defended these heights, while Cleburne's Division occupied

Right: *A battery of Federal light artillery at Chattanooga.*

the far right of the Confederate line, holding a heavily-fortified position that dominated the eastern approaches to Chattanooga. Immediately south of the city lay Hardee's smaller corps, deployed in the flat ground behind Chattanooga Creek, which lay between Missionary Ridge to the east and Lookout Mountain to the west. Finally, the Confederate garrison on Lookout Mountain lay on the western end of the Confederate line, a position that formed part of Hardee's deployment area. He considered the mountain to be too steep to climb except by the road that wound up its eastern face. If the position was attacked, Hardee would be able to send reinforcements to safeguard

Above: The 1851 *pattern Union artillery officer's stamped brass insignia, worn on the hat.*

the position long before any attacker could toil up the near-vertical slope on the western face of the mountain. Safe behind these formidable defensive positions, Bragg was content to wait and let the enemy come to him.

By mid-November, Grant was ready. His plan was deceptively simple. It called for Hooker to make a diversionary probe against the western slopes of Lookout Mountain to the west of the city, while Thomas did the same in front of Missionary Ridge to the southeast of the city. In theory this would pin the Confederates in their positions, leaving Sherman free to maneuver. The four divisions from the Union Army of the Tennessee that constituted XV and XVII Corps were encamped on the north bank of the river. Grant's plan called for these troops to cross the Tennessee to the northeast of the city, and then to attack the Missionary Ridge position in the flank, where the Confederate line was held by Cleburne. With luck he would capture the end of the ridge, and would then be in a position

Right: *A view of a section of Missionary Ridge, Chattanooga, as seen from the lowland over which Thomas's veterans advanced on November 25th.*

Above: *Looking towards Orchard Knob from Missionary Ridge.*

to work his way south down its length, attacking the Confederates in the flank and rolling up their line. It was a bold plan, and a lot depended on Bragg failing to react to Grant's maneuvers.

The battle began on November 23rd. Thomas led his army out of Chattanooga to attack a large knoll that overlooked his defenses. This was vital in order to give him space to deploy his army in the flat ground between the city and Missionary Ridge beyond it. His men captured "Orchard Knob" without much effort, as it lay beyond the main Confederate line, and was therefore only lightly defended. Thomas then deployed the three corps of his army. Palmer's

XIV Corps and Granger's IV Corps formed into line to the southeast of Orchard Knoll, while Howard's XX Corps provided the reserve, deployed east of the city where he could support either Thomas or Sherman. The first part of Grant's plan was complete. The following morning, Hooker launched his two corps against Lookout Mountain. Mist hung over the valley floor that morning, obscuring the movement of his troops from the defenders above. After Thomas' attack the day before, Hardee sent Brigadier-General Stevenson's Division to reinforce the gunners on top of Lookout Mountain. These defenders were surprised to see Union soldiers appearing out of the mist below them, scrambling up the side of the mountain. They had considered their position to be impregnable, but although the approach up the western slope was difficult it was not impossible. It was also too steep to allow the artillery batteries on top of the mountain to fire on the assaulting Union troops, so it was left to Stevenson's men to hold the position. The ground was so rugged on top of the mountain that the terrain protected the attackers, much as it did the defenders. Although they were outnumbered by four-to-one, the Confederates held the crest throughout the morning, encouraged by Breckinridge who appeared to help galvanize the defense. The fighting continued until nightfall, when the remaining Confederates withdrew to the south. Thanks to the mist that covered Hooker's attack, the battle for Lookout Mountain would erroneously be referred to as "The battle above the clouds."

The stage was now set for Sherman. He attacked at dawn on November 25th, his four divisions deployed in a deep line immediately to the west of Cleburne's position on Tunnel Hill, the northeastern end of Missionary Ridge.

Sherman's attacks continued all day, but the "Stonewall of the West" refused to budge. It was clear that Grant's great plan was failing. What followed was an example of the improvisation that helped Grant to outmaneuver Robert E. Lee the following summer. While the battle raged on his left, Thomas' Army of the Cumberland remained in position, save for Howard's Corps, which had been dispatched to

Above: *A period engraving of the battle for Lookout Mountain.*

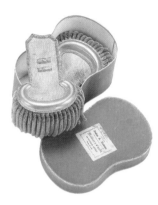

Above: A Federal infantry
lieutenant's epaulettes.

support Sherman. Grant was concerned that Cleburne might be reinforced from the unengaged Confederate center, and could then launch a counterattack against Sherman's battered divisions. He ordered Thomas to advance to pin the enemy to his front, and to drive the Confederates from their entrenched line at the foot of Missionary Ridge. At 3.30pm the 25,000 men of Palmer's and Granger's corps stepped forward, and within an hour they had succeeded in overrunning the forward line of the Confederate defenses. Although they outnumbered the defenders above them by two-to-one, Grant and Howard had no intention of storming the heights. That decision was made by the soldiers themselves, who continued their advance up the western slope of Missionary Ridge. Already demoralized by the retreat of the skirmishers lining the forward positions at the base of the ridge, the defenders became unsettled when Thomas' men advanced up the slope towards them. Despite the efforts of both Bragg and Breckinridge, the Confederates broke and ran. The divisions of Bates and Stewart simply dissolved, while those of Anderson further to the right held their ground until pressed, then they too joined the rout. Only Cleburne remained, but his heroic defense of Tunnel Hill had left him isolated. Unable to hold off both Sherman and Thomas, Cleburne withdrew, his troops forming the rearguard of the Confederate Army as it retreated.

The debacle at Chickamauga had been avenged by the Union. The three days of fighting had cost Grant 6,000 men, while Bragg had lost a similar number, of which 4,000 were prisoners mostly captured on Lookout Mountain and Missionary Ridge. Bragg's Army of Tennessee had been driven from Tennessee, and worse, it had lost the initiative to the enemy. Grant and Sherman would make sure the Confederates never regained it.

Left: *Major-General Joseph "Fighting Joe" Hooker on Lookout Mountain.*

Atlanta
June 27–September 1, 1864

Atlanta was a vital industrial center for the Confederacy, and Sherman's "total war" campaign of 1864 signaled it out as a key target. The battle for the city began on July 20. Despite a stiff defense by Joseph Johnston and John B. Hood, on the night of August 31 Hood was forced to flee. Sherman entered the city on September 2; when his forces left in mid-November, the city was in flames. Atlanta's Civil War heritage is today preserved by the Kennesaw Mountain National Battlefield site, which covers some 2,888 acres.

Right: *Confederate works in front of Atlanta; their munitions center was lost after months of hard fighting.*

Three days after his defeat on Missionary Ridge, Bragg asked President Davis to be relieved of his command, and his offer was willingly accepted. The unfortunate Bragg was replaced by the highly respected General Joseph E. Johnston, the man who had first opposed McClellan's Army of the Potomac in the Virginia Peninsula. His battered army consisted of around 30,000 men, divided into two corps, those of major-generals Hardee and Hood, but during the winter fresh drafts of troops raised the strength of the Army of Tennessee to almost 50,000 men. This total included the cavalry, a division of 5,000 men commanded by the spirited Major-General Wheeler. After his success at Chattanooga Grant reorganized the armies under his command. Thomas retained command of the Army of the Cumberland, while Sherman assumed control of the Union Army of the Tennessee. A smaller force, the Army of the Ohio was also released from garrison duty and brought forward to Chattanooga, where supplies and reinforcements were flooding in as preparations were made for the spring offensive. At the end of February Grant was recalled to Washington, and on March 8th he was given command of all Union forces, both in the Eastern and the Western Theaters. He elected to accompany the Army of the Potomac during the coming campaign, so he selected Sherman to replace him as the Union commander in the Western Theater. Grant knew he could rely on Sherman to pursue and destroy the enemy, and to steer the war to its conclusion in the West.

Sherman had 100,000 men at his disposal that spring: 60,000 in the Army of the Cumberland, 30,000 in the Army of the Tennessee, which was now commanded by Major-General McPherson, and finally another 14,000 men in the small Army of the Ohio, led by Major-General Schofield. His

intention was to use these troops to advance into Georgia, then drive through the mountains south of Chattanooga to reach Atlanta. With this vital city in Union hands, the Confederacy would be denied the ability to use their rail network, and the armies in the field would consequently wither away through lack of food and equipment. While Sherman outnumbered Johnston by two-to-one, the terrain worked in favor of the defenders, while Johnston was renowned as a highly-skilled defensive tactician.

Sherman began his advance on May 4th, almost the same time as Grant led the Army of the Potomac on its summer campaign in Virginia, its most strategically successful

Above: *Confederate defenses at Peach Tree Creek, an east-to-west flowing stream about three miles north of the city.*

Above: *Union Model* 1863
bayonet scabbard.

offensive in four years of fighting. Johnston's Confederate Army of Tennessee was deployed along the formidable Rocky Face Ridge, a feature that ran north–south and sat astride the railroad Sherman needed to move up his supplies, a few miles to the west of Dalton, Georgia. Unwilling to become bogged down in a costly frontal assault on the ridge, Sherman sent McPherson's Army of the Tennessee on a flank march around the left flank of the Confederate position. Meanwhile Thomas launched a series of probes designed to pin Johnston's army in place, so it would be unable to react to McPherson's flank march until it was too late. After passing through the line of mountains at Snake Creek Gap some eight miles south of Johnston's left flank, McPherson advanced to cut Johnston's supply line at Resaca, a small town ten miles south of Dalton. He expected to find the area devoid of troops, but instead he encountered a Confederate division, which held McPherson off until General Polk arrived with reinforcements, the rump of the Confederate Army of Mississsippi, which had just moved up from Alabama. It also allowed Johnston to withdraw from Dalton, and by May 13th he had concentrated his entire force around Resaca. With Polk's reinforcements he now commanded 60,000 men. Sherman brought the rest of his army up, and from May 13–15th he launched a series of assaults on the Confederate line—but failed to do anything more than incur heavy casualties. Johnston also lost 5,000 men during the fighting, and saw little point in continuing. On the evening of May 15th he withdrew south down the line of the Western and Atlantic Railroad, heading for the far more defensible position at Allatoona Pass.

Sherman managed to outmaneuver Johnston again, forcing him to abandon another strong position, and to fall

WILLIAM T. SHERMAN (1820–91)

Born in Ohio and raised by foster parents, William Sherman was sent to West Point, but spent the Mexican–American War on garrison duty in California. After a spell in civilian life, he rejoined the army as a Brigadier of Regulars, leading them into action at 1st Manassas. He was then sent west, and in October he was named as the commander of the Department of Kentucky. He was soon moved to the Department of the West, but his actions in hanging Confederate guerrillas led to his censure. He returned to field command in time to lead a division at Shiloh, and played a significant part in Grant's Vicksburg campaign as a corps commander. By September 1863 he had become the commander of the Army of the Tennessee, and led this force into action at Chattanooga. Grant came to rely on Sherman, and so when Grant was recalled to Washington to take command of the entire army, Sherman was named as overall commander in the West. Sherman's Atlanta Campaign was methodical, and he managed to maneuver the Confederates out of a series of strong defensive positions before isolating the city. Following its capture he sent part of his army north to fight Hood, while he led the remainder south towards Savannah on his infamous "March to the Sea". Once Georgia was secured he turned north, ravaging the Carolinas as he went, before finally bringing the last Confederate army to bay at Durham, North Carolina in April 1865. After the war he became general-in-chief of the army when Grant became President. Amidst a host of mediocre Union commanders, both Grant and Sherman stand out as true proponents of total war.

back once more. On May 25th Johnston made a stand at New Hope Church, near the small town of Dallas; this time Thomas launched a frontal attack, and was bloodily repulsed for his efforts. Two days later he attacked with Howard's Corps, but it too was badly mauled by Cleburne, who held the Confederate right. Clearly frontal attacks were not the answer, so Sherman sent McPherson in another outflanking march, and once again he forced Johnston to withdraw in order to protect his lines of communications. By the start of June Johnston had reached Kennesaw Mountain, just 30 miles from Atlanta. This time he was determined to hold his ground; the Confederates manhandled artillery to the summit, and built a formidable line of earthworks stretching some four miles along the ridge. While this work was underway Johnston held a forward line running just south of the railroad halt of Big Shanty, but Sherman was slow in following up, and it was mid-June before he reached Johnston's position. His batteries began a bombardment of the Confederate positions at Line Mountain, some two miles west of the railroad, and on June 14th a deliberately aimed shot resulted in the death of General Polk, one of Johnston's most experienced subordinates. While the soldiers were used to men being cut down in their hundreds, the deliberate targeting of Polk seemed unforgivable. Five days later Johnston pulled back to Kennesaw Mountain, and waited for Sherman's assault. It came on June 27th, after an outflanking maneuver by the Army of the Ohio was halted by Hood at Kolb's Farm, a few miles south of the main Confederate position. Sherman and his men were now wary of Johnston's ability to find good defensive terrain to hold, and Kennesaw was probably the most formidable line he

had occupied so far in the campaign. Sherman ordered McPherson to make a diversionary attack on the right of the Confederate line, while Thomas launched the main assault an hour later further to the south. The Union troops advanced in a series of waves, and when one was repulsed

Above: *Confederate palisades and chevaux-de-frise at Potter House. Despite such formidable looking earthworks, the city would be abandoned.*

another seemed to follow immediately behind it. Some Confederates complained their rifles were red hot from firing, but the wall of fire they created served its purpose. No Union soldiers got to within 15 yards of the Confederate line. The battle was reminiscent of Fredericksburg, where a series of wasteful frontal attacks broke against an impregnable Confederate position. Sherman broke off the

attack during the afternoon after suffering over 3,000 casualties. Unable to break Johnston's Army by assault, Sherman would have to find a way to maneuver him from his position.

By this time Sherman's men were used to their commander's fondness for flank marches. Schofield's Army of the Ohio made another wider flank march, and this time

Left: *Union officers at Atlanta. They include Brigadier-General Jefferson C. Davis, Commander of Sherman's 14th Corps in the Atlanta campaign and on the march through Georgia (front, far left); and Brigadier-General John Milton Brannan (front, third from left), Chief of artillery of the Army of the Cumberland, who was in charge of Union defenses at Atlanta after the occupation.*

Above: *Federal powder flask. Even this late in the day, such antiquated accoutrements were still in use.*

it succeeded in moving round behind Johnston, forcing him back through Marietta. Sherman then split his army into four columns, sending Thomas down through Marietta towards the rail crossing over the Chattahoochee River, while Schofield cut through the mountains to cross the river further to the east. McPherson's Army of the Tennessee was divided into two corps-sized columns, one supported by the bulk of Sherman's cavalry. The smaller force marched to the west of Thomas, where it threatened to turn the flank of any Confederate line north of the river. The cavalry accompanied the rest of the Army of the Tennessee to Roswell, crossed the river, then rode south to cut the railroad leading into Atlanta from the east. It was a masterly operation, as it denied Johnston the use of the river line that would otherwise have become a formidable defensive obstacle. By July 10th the Confederate army was south of the river, the bulk of it taking up a position three miles north of Atlanta on a ridge behind Peach Tree Creek. Other detachments were sent to protect Atlanta, and to shadow the Union forces approaching the city from the northeast. Johnston then waited for Thomas' Army of the Cumberland, allowing Sherman to move his whole army safely across the Chattahoochee River. President Davis became tired of all these retreats and missed opportunities, so on July 17th he ordered Hood to replace Johnston as commander of the Army of Tennessee. With the benefit of hindsight, this was probably a grave mistake. Hood was as rash as Johnston was cautious, and he wasted no time in going onto the offensive. On July 20th he launched an attack against Thomas' army at Peach Tree Creek, in an attempt to surprise the Union force as it was crossing. The Army of the Cumberland was sent reeling, and once more it looked as if it might be defeated by the Army of

Tennessee—but fate again intervened to spare it from destruction at the last minute. McPherson's Army marched to the sound of the guns, forcing Hood to divert Cleburne's Division to block his advance. This deprived Hardee and Stewart's Corps of the fresh troops they needed to finish off Thomas' army, and the battle ended at nightfall, allowing Thomas to disengage and retire to safety.

Above: *Union infantrymen Frederick G. Cordes (left) and brother Henry Cordes. Henry's arm was amputated on the battlefield at Jonesborough. He was taken the 25 miles to Atlanta to recover.*

Two days later Hood struck again. He moved his army back into Atlanta, where it appeared to be ensconced behind a formidable series of earthworks. McPherson's Army of the Tennessee deployed to the west of the city, along the Georgia Railroad. On the evening of July 21st Hood led Hardee's Corps off to the south, then looped round to arrive behind the Union left flank shortly after noon the following day. McPherson had strung his army out in a line, his men building entrenchments a mile to the east of the Confederate line, which was held by Cheatham's Corps (formerly Hood's command). At 12.15pm Hardee launched his attack, smashing out of the woods to strike Major-General Dodge's' XVI Corps on the left of McPherson's line. The Union line began to be rolled up from south to north. Although the assault met with considerable success at the

start, McPherson was able to redeploy his reserves to slow Hardee down, and by mid-afternoon the attack had ground to a halt. Hood then ordered Cheatham to storm out of the Atlanta entrenchments to pin the Union line in place from the west. This brought on a fresh wave of heavy fighting all along the Union line, and Cheatham punched through the Union line in the north, sending McPherson's right flank into disarray. At that critical moment Sherman arrived at the head of seven brigades of reinforcements. He hurled them into the fight in the north, and by nightfall the Confederates had been driven out of the Union position. The Battle of Atlanta had resulted in a hard-won Union victory. Hardee disengaged during the night, and his troops returned to Atlanta. In two days Hood had lost 8,000 men, more casualties than Johnston had lost in almost three months of

Left: *"Destruction of the depots, public buildings, and manufactories at Atlanta, Georgia, November 15, 1864." After destroying the warehouses and railroad facilities, Sherman began his March to the Sea, with 62,000 men and Lincoln's blessing. "I can make Georgia howl" was his chilling promise.*

fighting. While Sherman lost 4,000 men, he could afford the casualties. Hood could not.

A week later, Hood saw another opportunity to attack the enemy, as it slowly tightening its grip around the city. Sherman had sent Thomas west and south of the city to cut its last rail link with the rest of Georgia. Thomas had assumed command of the Union Army of the Tennessee after McPherson was killed in battle on July 22nd. Major-General S.D. Lee had also replaced Cheatham, and on July 28th he attacked Howard's isolated force at Ezra Church, to the west of the city. Howard commanded two corps, and these men held their ground, forcing Lee to launch a series of costly frontal attacks, all of which were repulsed. This engagement cost Hood another 5,000 men, and his army was rapidly shrinking. He now had less than 35,000 men left compared to Sherman's 90,000. Finally Howard reached Jonesboro, some 14 miles south of Atlanta, cutting the Macon and Western Railroad. Hood marched south to meet them, hoping to isolate the Union force, and to defeat it before it could be reinforced. On August 31st he hurled Cleburne against Howard, but the Union commander had formed a strong defensive box with his flank protected by the Flint River, and Cleburne failed to break the Union perimeter. Hood then recalled S.D. Lee to Atlanta, leaving Hardee to continue the assault with just three divisions. During the morning of September 1st Thomas arrived with the Army of the Cumberland. During the day Thomas assaulted Hardee's line near Jonseboro, and by the afternoon Howard had come up to support him. With Thomas attacking from the north and Howard assaulting from the west, Hardee was unable to hold his position, and by nightfall he had been driven off to the southeast, leaving

Union troops in control of the railroad. Atlanta's last lifeline had been cut, and the city was now completely isolated. Hood had no alternative but to evacuate the city, after destroying what he could of its railroad facilities, to prevent them from falling into Sherman's hands. On September 2nd Sherman's troops marched into the abandoned city, and by the evening President Lincoln had received the news: "General Sherman has taken Atlanta." Time was now running out for the Confederacy.

Below: *Union artillery uniforms and equipment. the branch color, red, is clear. The short jackets were worn by horse artillery, the longer coats by foot artillery.*

Nashville
December 2–15, 1864

Nashville was the first Confederate industrial city to fall to Federal forces, and was captured on February 23, 1862. Hood's attempts to retake Nashville in December 1864 were repulsed by the numerically superior forces of Thomas and Schofield. They pursued the retreating Confederates, with only rearguard action saving Hood's force from total destruction. At present, no national battlefield exists at Nashville, though several historic sites relating to the battle are open to the public across the city, including Nashville National Cemetery.

Right: *Winter quarters of Sherman's troops duriing thier March to the Sea after the capture of Atlanta.*

After abandoning Atlanta on September 1st, Hood's Army of Tennessee was reduced to less than 35,000 men. He retreated southwest to Palmetto, a small town some 20 miles from Atlanta, and considered what he could do next. Numerically his army was now no match for Sherman, who outnumbered him by roughly three-to-one. Clearly a straightforward engagement was unthinkable, so instead Hood devised one of the most ambitious offensive plans of the war. He decided that by marching around Sherman's army and placing himself astride the Union Army's lines of communication, he would force Sherman to divide his force, and send detachments north to deal with the new Confederate threat. He might even be able to lure him away from Atlanta. On September 25th President Davis arrived at Hood's encampment, and after a lengthy meeting he approved the scheme that the general proposed to him, at least in principle. Having received approval for his operation, Hood broke camp and marched the Army of Tennessee west, crossing the Chattahoochee and then striking north through the mountains that Johnston had used to delay Sherman's advance. On October 1st he reached Allatoona, cutting the line of the Georgia Central Railroad. His men spent the next four days pulling up tracks and destroying telegraph cables. Inevitably Sherman reacted by sending part of his army north to secure his lines of communication. On October 6th Hood led his army west, crossing the Coosa River just west of the town of Rome, then looping north to fall on Resaca on October 12th. He demanded the surrender of the Union garrison in the town, but word had reached the defenders that Sherman was now marching north with his whole army, so they refused. Unwilling to be drawn into a protracted assault, Hood

moved off again to the north, entering Dalton on October 13th. Sherman advanced rapidly, and by the time Hood was at Dalton, his leading units were approaching Resaca. Warned of Sherman's approach, Hood moved off to the west towards Lafayette, 20 miles south of Chattanooga. On October 15th the Confederate rearguard fought a skirmish with Sherman's leading units at Snake Creek Gap, but Sherman was unable to delay Hood, who marched through Lafayette, then headed down to the southwest towards

Above: *During the seige, defending guns were practically on the steps of the state capitol on the hill . The trestle bridge was quickly assembled by Union troops to bring in men and matériel.*

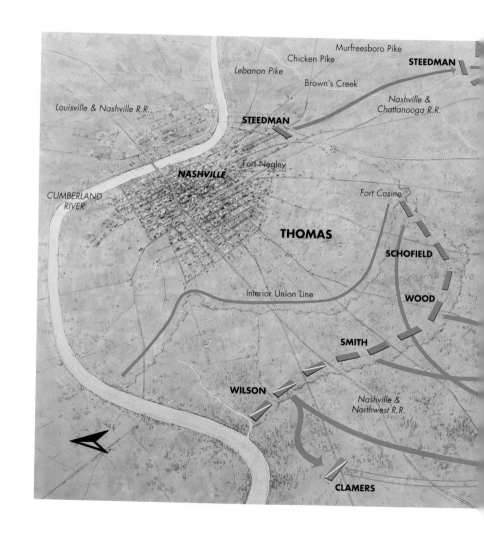

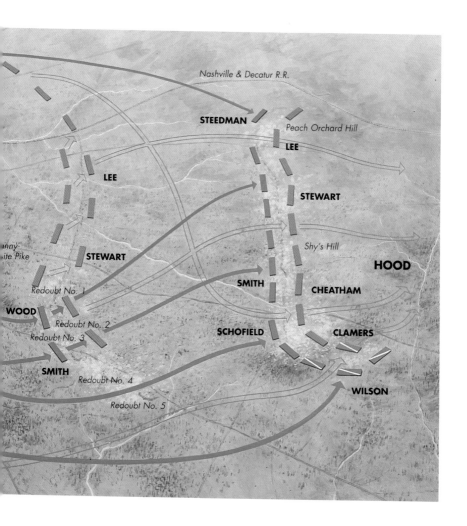

Nashville & Decatur R.R.

STEEDMAN

Peach Orchard Hill

LEE

LEE

STEWART

Shy's Hill

unny
ite Pike

STEWART

HOOD

Redoubt No. 1

SMITH

CHEATHAM

WOOD

Redoubt No. 2

Redoubt No. 3

SCHOFIELD

CLAMERS

SMITH

Redoubt No. 4

Redoubt No. 5

WILSON

Previous pages and below: *When Hood's attack stalled, Thomas (below) sent the cavalry to clear Charlotte Pike on December 15th, bottom center, while Steedman attacked Hook's right flank, who retreated to a line between the Franklin and Hillsboro pikes. On the 16th Wood and Smith struck the center and only a desperate rearguard action prevented encirclement and disaster, as Cheatham was turned on Shy's Hill.*

Gaylesville, just over the state line in Alabama. Sherman continued the pursuit as far as Gaylesville, by which time Hood was on the move again, heading deep into northern Alabama towards Gadsden on the Coosa River, 40 miles southwest of Gaylesville. Sherman had pursued Hood as far as Gaylesville, but that was just as far as he intended to go. He had already been humiliated by Hood, forced to march and countermarch his vastly superior army in pursuit of the Confederate force, and in the process he had all but abandoned Georgia. Tired of what he saw as a "wild goose chase," Sherman ordered Thomas' Army of the Cumberland and Schofield's Army of the Ohio to move north into Tennessee, which was now under threat from Hood's Army. Sherman would return to Georgia, where he planned to launch a whirlwind offensive of his own.

Hood was now far from any source of supply. At this point he developed a truly ambitious plan—though reckless might be a far more apt description of his scheme. He decided to advance north through Alabama into Tennessee. He would head north through Nashville into Kentucky, then move through Bowling Green to Louisville. Then he would follow the Ohio River east into the mountains, emerging in western Virginia, where he would be able to link up with Robert E. Lee's army. Clearly Hood was a desperate man. The proposed venture was a logistical impossibility, and ignored the simple fact that while the Confederates lacked rail communications, Sherman and Grant could move troops virtually wherever they wanted in Tennessee and Kentucky, and would have little problem blocking his path with a superior force. Hood's aggressive spirit had brought the army to the edge of destruction at Atlanta. He would finish the job in Tennessee. After leaving Gadsten in mid-October, he marched northwest towards Guntersville on the Tennessee River, then followed the river downstream to Decatur. By this time Union river patrols had informed Sherman where Hood was, and it was clear Hood was attempting to cross the river and extend his diversion into Tennessee, as Sherman had anticipated. Consequently Schofield moved the 28,000-strong Army of the Ohio to cover the border near Pulaski, Tennessee, while Thomas remained on the line of the Nashville and Chattanooga Railroad with his 30,000 men of the Army of the Cumberland. The plan was to combine the two forces, then crush Hood in central Tennessee. The Confederate Army reached Decatur, Alabama on October 26th, but found the city too heavily fortified to risk an assault. Unable to cross the Tennessee River at Decatur, Hood marched his army downstream to Tuscumbia. His

Below: *Following the bloody failure at Nashville, General John B. Hood asked to be relieved in January and saw no more active service.*

vanguard arrived in the city on October 30th, but Hood waited for another 19 days before he led his army across the river, hoping that reinforcements and stragglers would boost his numbers, which were already falling due to desertion and sheer exhaustion. By November 18th the army was on the march again, heading north through Athens along the line of the Nashville and Decatur Railroad. Schofield fell back ahead of him, and Hood entered Tennessee without opposition. By November 26th Hood was approaching Columbia, where Schofield had decided to halt and make a stand. However, Hood circled round the city, crossing the Duck River a few miles to the east, and turning Schofield's position. The Army of the Ohio fell back to the north towards Spring Hill and Franklin. Hood hoped to cut off Schofield's retreat at Spring Hill, but the Union columns were able to use the better road surface of the Franklin and Columbia Turnpike, and passed Spring Hill before Hood arrived. Hood followed in pursuit of Schofield, and ten miles further on he found him. The Union commander had halted in front of the small city of Franklin. His position was a strong one, his line curving back on both flanks to meet the Harpeth River. Hood would have to launch a frontal assault if he was going to attack at all. A more cautious commander might have hesitated; Hood only had 22,000 men left under his command, divided into two corps. The 28,000 defenders were digging in, and the approaches to their positions were covered by artillery on both sides of the river. The time was now 3.30pm. Hood ordered Cheatham and Stewart to launch an immediate attack against Schofield's left flank. 20,000 Confederates charged forward, engulfing two Union brigades that were deployed in front of the main line of entrenchments. These

units were swept away, and the attackers carried on to the line of earthworks beyond. The attackers managed to push the defenders back, but then the Union troops held their ground on the outskirts of the town. Schofield launched a counterattack, which drove the Confederates back to the entrenchments, and despite brutal hand-to-hand fighting,

Above: *Once this impressive trestle bridge was up near Whiteside, VA, nothing would slow the Union supplies streaming along the Nashville and Chattanooga Railroad.*

Right: *The 8th Wisconsin Volunteer Infantry bought their mascot, "Old Abe", for $2.50. Not surprisingly, they became known as the Eagle Regiment. A courageous and reliable soldier appointed as "eagle bearer" would carry Old Abe on a specially constructed perch between the 8th Wisconsin's national color and state color, in the center. The Eagle regiment fought with particular distinction at Vicksburg, and Old Abe was in the thick of it at Nashville. He would see out the war, having survived at least 36 engagements.*

Hood's men were unable to regain the initiative. Schofield pulled out of Franklin under cover of darkness, and the Confederates were too exhausted to stop him. The battle was a bloody affair. Hood lost 6,000 men killed and wounded, the casualties including no less than 12 generals, one of them being the irreplaceable Cleburne.

After the bloodbath at Franklin, Hood continued his march north towards Nashville. This time his opponent would be Major-General Thomas, whose 30,000-strong Army of the Cumberland was entrenching on the southern edge of the city. Late on December 1st Schofield's force joined him, bringing the strength of the army up to 54,000 men. If Hood wanted to cross the Cumberland River, he would have to fight his way through a Union army twice his size, protected by well-sited entrenchments and covered by large numbers of artillery pieces, including siege guns. The Confederate Army of Tennessee arrived in front of Nashville on December 2nd. It was obvious that the Union position was too strong to assault, so Hood ordered his men to dig in a mile to the south of the city, while he decided what to do next. Any further operations were then halted by a spell of severe weather, including an ice storm that battered the area. Grant began badgering Thomas to attack Hood before he escaped again, but the commander of the Army of the Cumberland seemed reluctant to launch an assault. Finally Grant ordered him to launch an immediate attack, regardless of the weather. The Confederate position lay opposite the southeastern side of the city, as Hood had insufficient men to extend his line all the way around Nashville. Consequently the southwestern side of the city was screened by nothing more than a few Confederate cavalry patrols. Thomas decided to send Steedman's Division

forward to demonstrate against the Confederate front, while he led three corps southwest to attack the Confederates in the flank. Major-General Wood's IV Corps was ordered to storm Montgomery Hill at the left end of the Confederate line, while Schofield's XXIII Corps and Smith's XVI Corps passed the hill to attack the line of redoubts that covered the Confederate left flank and rear. Meanwhile the Union cavalry under Major-General Wilson would follow on behind,

Left: *The 34th Massachusetts on parade two years previously. A month before Nashville, these men would face another Confederate offensive, in the Shenandoah Valley at Cedar Creek. The surprise attack nearly succeeded, had it not been for Sheridan's personal arrival. It is extraordinary that the Confederate Army had the spirit to go on the offensive at the end of 1864, either in the Valley, or across the Mississippi as they did under General Sterling Price, or at Nashvillle: but Nashville would be the last.*

ready to ride into the enemy if they broke. By the morning of December 15th everything was ready, and Thomas launched his attack at noon. A severe ice storm covered the Union approach, and the Confederates were unable to react to the attack before Thomas' Army was upon them. Stewart's Corps bore the brunt of the attack, but it was deployed to face an attack coming from the north, not the west. The defenders were also heavily outnumbered. The attackers succeeded in capturing Montgomery Hill after a tough fight, and the line of four redoubts to the south of this key position. Hood tried to rush troops to plug the gap in his left flank, moving part of Cheatham's Corps from his unengaged right, but it was not enough to hold off the attackers. By late-afternoon the Confederates had been pushed back to the south, where Hood rallied his army in a line stretched between two hills; Shy's Hill on the left, and Overton Hill on the right, two miles away to the east. This bought the Confederates some time, but it was not enough to stem the "blue tide."

After regrouping his army during the night, Thomas prepared for a fresh assault in the mid-afternoon of December 16th. He gave the order at 3.30pm, launching Schofield's Corps against Cheatham's depleted ranks on the Confederate left. While Smith and Wood launched pinning attacks against the Confederate center and right, the massed assault against Hood's left wing swept the defenders from Shy's Hill. Hood's army dissolved as panic seized the Army of Tennessee. The veterans who had been through so much had finally had enough. Hood managed to form a rearguard, which kept Wilson's Union cavalry at bay, and the surviving Confederates streamed south through the ice and snow. Hood rallied what was left of his army at Tupelo, Mississippi, but of the 35,000 men who had left Georgia in September, barely half that number remained under arms. He had lost at least 5,500 men at Nashville, while another 4,500 were taken prisoner. His army was effectively finished as a fighting force. On January 23rd Hood was stripped of his command, and the remnants of his army were taken back to Georgia, which was being systematically ravaged by Sherman's Army as it marched from Atlanta to the sea. Hood's defeat at Nashville meant there could now no longer be any hope for the

confederacy. The Battle of Nashville was not brilliantly executed by Thomas: he took too long to launch his attacks and lost some of his great advantage in numbers. It was, however, a resounding victory, and a cutoff point. Hood had only been at Nashville because he had nowhere else to go. Although the Confederate Army of Tennessee would fight again, all it was doing was postponing the inevitable.

Below: *Confederate artillery uniforms and equipment; compare this with page 231. As in other branches, equipment used by the Rebel artillery was often captured, like the* Model 1833 US Foot Artillery sword.

EPILOG

The war did not officially end that Christmas after Nashville, and Lee's surrender at Appomattox lay four months away. In between the South would suffer even further, and the killing would continue. On November 15, 1864 General Sherman rode out of the smoking ruins of Atlanta with 62,000 hard-worn soldiers. He drove them down through Georgia to the sea, burning and destroying everything that could aid the Confederacy; railroads, plantation houses, mills and crops. The Republican victory in the November elections gave President Lincoln his second term, and Sherman was ordered to do whatever he considered necessary to deprive the Confederacy of the materials and will to continue the fight. The Union General coined the phrase; "war is hell," and he proceeded to demonstrate the axiom by visiting destruction on anything in his path. A growing number of freed slaves accompanied the army as it marched, adding to the devastation by way of revenge. On December 10th Sherman reached the outskirts of Savannah, and ten days later the city fell to his troops. Sherman could now be supplied by the Union Navy, and he continued northwards into the Carolinas. The Confederates had no army left with which to oppose him. A force of Georgia militia had attacked his army at Macon, Georgia, but the raw troops proved no match for Sherman's veterans. Major-General Hardee had scraped together whatever troops he could, and by February the survivors from Nashville had been shipped to the coast. The two forces combined with a division of reinforcements led by D.H. Hill and a handful of cavalry under Wheeler, and the various

Above: Identification badge of Col. P. J. Yorke, Bayards Brigade, 1st Pennsyslvania Cavalry. The !st Pennsylvania first saw action on December 20, 1861, at Drainesville, and mustered out on September 1, 1864. In between lay 1st and 2nd Mannassas, then Fredericksburg, Gettysburg, and many other battles and skirmishes.

contingents were reorganized into a new Army of Tennessee. With barely 17,000 troops in the army, General Beauregard could do little to stop Sherman's advance. On February 17th the Union army razed Columbia, South Carolina, and within days Charleston had fallen. The capture of Wilmington in late-November meant that the few remaining Confederates were cut off from the outside world, and from any supplies. Beauregard was joined by General Johnston, his joint commander at 1st Manassas. This time Johnston assumed command, and led the Army of Tennessee into action one more time at Bentonville, North Carolina on March 19, 1865. It was a last-ditch attempt to harm a victorious enemy, and

Below: *The ruins of the Confederate capital, Richmond; what was not leveled by the Federal artillery or destroyed by the evacuating Confederates was razed by the fire.*

Below: *Fort Sumter, in the center of Charleston Harbor, South Carolina. The first shot of the war had been fired here on April 12th, 1861 at 4.30 a.m. Exactly four years later the Union flag would be raised here amid great celebrations.*

Sherman's men were surprised, but they rallied. Eventually the Union's superiority in numbers made itself felt, and the Confederates withdrew to the north. Sherman would pursue Johnston's broken army. Two weeks later the Army of the Potomac broke through the Confederate lines at Petersburg, and Lee began the week-long retreat that would end at Appomattox Court House.

After Lee's surrender at Appomatox Court House on April 9th the fighting was officially drawn to a close in Virginia, but it continued for another week further to the south, until Johnston surrendered the Army of Mississippi on April 17th, and with it the remaining states in the Confederacy. Word of the surrender would take longer to reach Confederate outposts further afield, but the fighting had ceased.

By that time President Lincoln had been assassinated, and any calls for moderation were swept away. The South would pay dearly for the death of Lincoln in the years that followed, and the retribution started immediately. On April 23rd the conciliatory surrender terms signed by Sherman and Johnston would be repudiated, and for a decade the already ravaged South would suffer the indignities of military rule, reparations and political disenfranchisement.

However, what remained was the sacrifice made by the men of both sides for their respective causes. Eventually the country would be reborn, and the hardship and heroism experienced by both sides would be acknowledged as a tool from which a new and stronger nation could emerge. The United States of America we know today may have been created in 1775, but it came of age during the span of these five blood-soaked Aprils between 1861 and 1865. Its importance is manifest in the battle sites preserved, and the monuments that can be found across the country.

Below: *May 1865, and the crowds look down Pennsylvania Avenue toward the Washington Capitol to see the sixth Corps of the Army of the Republic parading past.*

BATTLE SITE INFORMATION

The majority of the major Civil War battlefield sites are now owned in part by the National Park Service, part of the US Department of the Interior. In most cases they provide an interpretation center, and own a portion of the land on which the battle was fought. They provide superb guided walks, while self-guided walking and automobile tour routes are also provided. Details of the principal National Park Service centers are provided below, or can be accessed through the NPS website, http://www.nps.gov The website also provides information on how to reach the battlefields, opening times of the interpretation centers and gift stores, and information for teachers, parents and group leaders to help them plan their visit. In addition most areas include additional sites of interest to the visitor, including locations of relevant sites outside the NPS boundaries. For example, the Virginia Civil War Trails network provides an extensive series of interpretative markers showing where crucial events took place, and a tour of these in conjunction with a visit to the National Park Service sites will give the visitor a better understanding of the flow of a campaign or battle. Most Visitor Centers sell guides to these sites including the excellent *The Official Virginia Civil War Battlefield Guide*, while similar publications cover sites in other States.

EASTERN THEATER SITES

Manassas

The Manassas National Battlefield Park is located on the site of two major Civil War battles, and is located a few miles north of Manassas, Virginia.

The site encompasses some 5,000 acres, and is one of the best preserved sites in the country in terms of presenting a largely unaltered battlefield to visit. The substantial Henry House Hill Visitor Center includes a museum, a film auditorium and a book and gift store.
Website: http://www.nps.gov/mana

Getting there:

From Washington D.C. take Interstate 66 West to Exit 47B, then Business Route 234 North. Proceed through the first traffic light, then take the second right to the Henry Hill Visitor Center, which is located at the top of the hill. In addition the Stuart's Hill Center Facilities include a small museum, but this secondary site is only open at weekends during the summer. It is located at the intersection of Route 29 and Pageland Lane.

The Seven Days Battles

The Richmond National Battlefield Park is located in the old Tredegar Ironworks in its old riverfront location downtown Richmond, although the Park includes a number of remote sites and interpretative facilities, including park areas at Beaver Dam Creek, Gaines Mill, Cold Harbor, Glendale, Malvern Hill and Drewry's Bluff. The Richmond headquarters is the natural starting point of a tour of either the Peninsular Campaign battlefields of 1862, or Grant's Summer Campaign battlefields of 1864. The Tredegar Center contains a large and impressive museum, plus a gift store, a computerized interpretative facility, a film auditorium and a tour of the Tredaegar industrial facility. A series of self-guided or occasional guided tours are available at each of the battle

sites, while self-drive tape tours are also available.
Website: http://www.nps.gov/rich/

Getting there:

Traveling north on I-95: take exit 74C west then follow signs to Civil War Visitor Center located at 490 Tredegar Street. Traveling South on I-95: use exit 75 for Civil War Visitor Center. From there, Park Rangers will provide all the information you need about visiting the other locations in the Richmond National Battlefield Park.

Antietam

The Antietam National Battlefield, Maryland encompasses the main areas of the battlefield, including the Cornfield, Dunker Church, the West Woods, the Sunken Lane and Burnside's Bridge. The Visitor Center is located near the Dunker Church on the outskirts of Sharpsburg, and leaflets and tapes are provided for self-guided walking or automobile tours, while a series of well-informed tours by Park Rangers are also provided using the Center as a base. The facilities also include a small museum, a film auditorium, a gift store and an observation deck, which provides a good all-weather view of the battlefield.
Website: http://www.nps.gov/anti/

Getting there:

From Interstate 70 take exit 29 if heading west or exit 29A if heading east. Follow Route 65 south for ten miles and turn off at the Visitor Center.

Fredericksburg & Spotsylvania

The Fredericksburg & Spotsylvania National Military Park, Virginia is based at the foot of Marye's Heights on the southern edge of Fredericksburg, while an additional smaller center is located on the Spotsylvania site. The Fredericksburg facility includes a small museum, a good gift store and provides the starting point for guided tours by Park Rangers along the line of the stone wall which anchored the Confederate defence. Additional self-guided tour routes are provided around both battlefields, and encompass several additional sites of Civil War interest.
Website: http://www.nps.gov/frsp/

Getting there:

If coming from Washington D.C. to Fredericksburg on Interstate 95, take the Route 3 east exit, then drive east for approximately 2 miles until you reach a traffic light at the intersection of Route 3 (also called the Blue and Gray Parkway) with Business Route 1 (also called Lafayette Blvd.). Turn left and drive approximately 1/2 mile, and the Visitor Center will be on your left. If driving north from Richmond on I-95, take the Fredericksburg exit, then drive about 1 mile on U.S. 1 (also called Jefferson Davis Highway) to a traffic light where US 1 splits. Bear right on Business Route 1, Lafayette Blvd, then drive about 4 miles to the Visitor Center which is on the left.

Gettysburg

The Gettysburg National Military Park is probably the largest battlefield interpretation center in the country, located on the top of Cemetery Ridge immediately behind the area held by Meade's Union army. It comprises an extensive museum (based around the George Rosenteel Collection), a superb gift store and bookshop, a film auditorium an "electric map" and a cyclorama, where visitors are presented with an interpretation of a battlefield painting "in the round". Frequent re-enactment events are staged at the Center, while numerous Park Ranger-

guided tours are provided. The Center also serves as a base for self-guided walking or driving tours of the battlefields, while numerous retail sites in the town of Gettysburg will prove of interest to the visitor. The battlefield is dotted with monuments, artillery pieces and interpretative markers. Licenced battlefield tour guides are also available to provide you with your own personal tour.
Websites: http://www.nps.gov/gett
http://www.gettysburgtourguides.org/

Getting there:
The National Park Service Visitor Center is located between the Taneytown Road (State Rt. 134) and Steinwehr Avenue (Bus. Rt. 15), a mile south of Gettysburg. Visitors traveling on U.S. Route 15 should follow the NPS signs which direct them to the Center. Visitors traveling west on State Rt. 30 should exit onto U.S. Route 15 South and follow the park signs. If approaching Gettysburg on State Rt. 30 traveling east, drive into town as far as Washington Street (third traffic light), then turn right. Continue along Washington Street for a mile (passing through two more lights) and the Visitor Center will be on the right.

Chancellorsville and the Wilderness
Part of the Fredericksburg and Spotsylvania National Military Park, the Chancellorsville Battlefield Visitor Center is the starting point for any tour of both of the battles fought in the Wilderness in 1863–64. It is located yards from the site where "Stonewall" Jackson received his fatal wound at the heighnt of the Battle of Chancellorsville. Facilities include a small museum and film auditorium, and a small gift store and bookshop. Park Ranger guided tours are provided at various locations around the battlefield, while guides are provided to assist those who which to tour the battlefields by car, or on self-guided walking tours.
Website: http://www.nps.gov/frsp/cville.htm

Getting there:
From Interstate 95 head west towards Culpeper on Route 3 for six miles. The Chancellorsville Battlefield Visitor is signposted a mile beyond the site of the Chancellorsville House, on the right side of the road. The Wilderness interpretative shelters are located further to the west, and can be found via the website, or by the map provided at the Visitor Center.

The Siege of Petersburg
The Petersburg National Military Park is located on the south side of the city, close to the old Confederate siege lines, and the scene of some of the heaviest fighting of the siege. It comprises the usual National Park Service facilities, including a film auditorium, a gift store and an interpretative center. Park Ranger guided tours are provided, while the NPS also maintains satellite stations at City Point (the site of Grant's Headquarters), at the Five Forks Battlefield, and at the Poplar Grove Cemetery. A self-guided automobile tour is recommended, as the tour incorporates some 26 miles of sites.
Website: http://www.nps.gov/pete/

Getting There:
Take the Wythe Street (Rt. 36 east) exit from Interstate 95, then follow the road some 2.5 miles to the Visitor Center, which is located on the right. Alternatively, if arriving via Interstate 295, take exit 9B onto Rt. 36, then drive west to the Vistor Center, located on the right just past Fort Lee.

Western Theater Sites

Shiloh

The Shiloh National Military Park consists of 4,000 acres, encompassing most of the crucial areas where the two-day battle was fought in 1862. The Center located near Pittsburg Landing boasts an extensive and well-organized museum, a film auditorium and a gift store and bookshop. A number of Park Ranger tours leave from the Center, while facilities are also provided for self-guided tours along hiking trails, or by car. The battlefield itself contains numerous markers and interpretative displays at key locations.
Website: http://www.nps.gov/shil/

Getting There:

From Interstate 40 exit at Lexington Tennessee, then take Highway 22 South to the Visitor Center. If traveling south from Memphis, take Highway 57 East, then Highway 22 North.

Murfreesbro

The Stones River National Battlefield incorporates nearby Fort Rosencrans, and encompasses some 600 acres on the western side of Murfreesbro. The small Visitor Center has a display and slide show in their interpretative centre, and a gift store. Daily Park Ranger tours are provided, and information is available for those wishing to conduct self-guided tours of the battlefield. Fort Rosencrans was built after the battle, but is a superb example of a Civil War-era earthwork field fortification.
Website: http://www.nps.gov/stri/index.htm

Getting There:

From Interstate 24 take exit 78B, then follow Highway 96 to the intersection with U.S. Highway 41/70. Turn left and take Highway 41/70 north to Thompson Lane. Turn left onto Thompson Lane, then follow the signs to the Old Nashville Highway and the Visitor Center.

Siege of Vicksburg

The Vicksburg National Military Park is an extensive site, providing a high level of interpretation. The Visitor Center itself contains one of the best Civil War museums around, with displays covering siegeworks, medical facilities, and life inside the besieged city. The center also boasts a film auditorium and a good gift store and bookshop. Nearby is the USS Cairo Museum, where the remains of a Civil War Union ironclad are displayed, alongside an interpretation centre covering the naval war on the Mississippi. Finally the battlefield site itself contains trails, and both Park Ranger and self-guided tour facilities are available.
Website: http://www.nps.gov/vick/

Getting There:

From the east (Jackson, Mississippi), take Interstate 20 west to Vicksburg, then take exit 4B. Follow Clay Street (US-80) west for 1/4 mile to reach the park entrance.

Chickamauga and Chattanooga

The Chickamauga and Chattanooga National Military Park is located in the area defended by General Thomas, the "Rock of Chickamauga" during the battle in 1863, while additional park facilities cover the fighting around Chattanooga to the north. An additional Visitor Center is located on the top of Lookout Mountain, but this center is one of the least impressive NPS facilities on this list, lacking (at the time of the author's last visit) both the usual professional Park Ranger staff willing to help visitors, and the normal extensive interpretative facilities available

in most larger Visitor Centers. By contrast the Chickamauga Visitor Center is a well-maintained site, with an extremely good museum, film auditorium and gift store. Park Ranger tours and self-guided walking tour routes are provided, but the best way to see the battlefield is by self-guided car tour.
Website: http://www.nps.gov/chch/

Getting There:
Chickamauga Visitor Center is located a mile south of the intersection of Highway 2 (Battlefield Parkway) and Highway 27 at Fort Oglethrope, Georgia. Lookout Mountain Battlefield Visitor Center is located on East Brow Road on the top of Lookout Mountain, above Chattanooga, Tennessee.

Atlanta

Two major interpretative centers are provided in the Atlanta area; the Kennesaw Mountain National Battlefield Park, and the Atlanta Cyclorama. In addition the Atlanta History Center located near the site of the Battle of Peach Tree Creek includes a superb Civil War display, and the museum contains a number of artifacts related to the battle for the city in 1864. The Kennesaw Mountain Visitor Center has a small museum and audio-visual display, and a small giftstore. Ranger talks are available, but in order to tour the Kennesaw battlefield you need a car, as the siege lines are fairly extensive. The Atlanta Cyclorama and Civil War Museum is well worth a vistit, as it houses a painting "in the round" similar to that owned by the National Park Service in their Gettysburg Cyclorama.
Websites: http://www.nps.gov/kemo/
http://www.webguide.com/cyclorama.html
http://www.atlantahistorycenter.com/
http://www.atlantaga.gov/

Getting There:
Kennesaw: Take I-75 to exit 269 (Barrett Parkway). At the light turn West onto Barrett Parkway. Travel down Barrett Parkway for approximately 3 miles, turn left at the light, onto Old Hwy 41. Turn right at your next light, Stilesboro Rd. The Visitor Center will be immediately on your left. For the other attractions, see their web sites, or the site provided by the City of Atlanta which covers transportation within the city.

Nashville

No battlefield interpretation centre is available on this site, although a visit to any of the National Park Service Bookshops will provide information useful to the visitor who wishes to conduct a self-guided tour of the now fully built-over site.

The Blue and the Gray
Francis Miles Finch (1827-1907)
stanzas one and seven

By the flow of the inland river,
Whence the fleets of iron have fled,
Where the blades of the grave-grass quiver,
Asleep are the ranks of the dead:
Under the sod and the dew,
Waiting the Judgment Day:
Under the one, the Blue,
Under the other, the Gray.

No more shall the war-cry sever,
Or the winding rivers be red;
They banish our anger forever
When they laurel the graves of our dead!
Under the sod and the dew,
Waiting the Judgment Day:
Love and tears for the Blue,
Tears and love for the Gray.